May this
Bless your Reno,
Bed, Prayer, & Intimacy
like never Before?

Christy

Sex
Let the Church Say, Amen!

A Practical Approach on How to Access and Fight for a Great Sex Life in Your Christian Marriage

Christy Jewell Kirkland

WestBow
PRESS
A DIVISION OF THOMAS NELSON

Copyright © 2011 Christy Jewell Kirkland

All rights reserved. No part of this book may be used or reproduced by any means, graphic, electronic, or mechanical, including photocopying, recording, taping or by any information storage retrieval system without the written permission of the publisher except in the case of brief quotations embodied in critical articles and reviews.

WestBow Press books may be ordered through booksellers or by contacting:

WestBow Press
A Division of Thomas Nelson
1663 Liberty Drive
Bloomington, IN 47403
www.westbowpress.com
1-(866) 928-1240

Because of the dynamic nature of the Internet, any web addresses or links contained in this book may have changed since publication and may no longer be valid. The views expressed in this work are solely those of the author and do not necessarily reflect the views of the publisher, and the publisher hereby disclaims any responsibility for them.

Any people depicted in stock imagery provided by Thinkstock are models, and such images are being used for illustrative purposes only.

Certain stock imagery © Thinkstock.

ISBN: 978-1-4497-1286-0 (sc)
ISBN: 978-1-4497-1287-7 (e)

Library of Congress Control Number: 2011922926

Scripture taken from the King James Version of the Holy Bible.

Printed in the United States of America

WestBow Press rev. date: 3/21/2011

Contents

Prologue	xv
Introduction	xxi

Ch. 1 Sex is Powerful 1
   Sex Can Injure You and Your Spouse 9
   Self-Inflicted Injuries 16

Ch. 2 Sex Has Many Advantages 25
   Sex Can Bring You and Your Spouse Closer both Naturally
   and Spiritually. 33
   Sex Brings Forth Children 37
   Sex Helps You Deal with Everyday Flesh and Temptations ... 42

Ch. 3 Common Misconceptions about Sex 53
   Sex is A Bad Word 53
   Sex is Nasty 54
   Sex is Not Beautiful in the Eyes of the Lord ... 57
   Sex is Not the Purpose of Marriage 58
   Sex Should Not Be Discussed in the Church Amongst Saints ... 61

Ch. 4 What Is All the Fighting About? 63
   The Enemy 70
   The Fight for Your Life 75

**Ch. 5 What Does Satan Want from Me? What Is His Strategy
in My Marriage?** 79
   Tactic 1: ANNIHILATION 79
   Tactic 2: BLINDSIDE YOU 82
   Tactic 3: CONTROL YOUR CONFESSION ... 89
   Tactic 4: DECEIVE AND DEFILE YOU 97

Ch. 6 The Rules of Engagement in Sex 107

Ch. 7 The Art of Building True Love 119

<u>Bonus Material</u>
His & Hers: 105 ways to spice up your sex life tonight!

To My Husband

This book is dedicated to the love of my life, my bishop; the lord of our home and a man who rules his house as well as his Spirit. You are truly a diamond in the rough. Grounded, secure, unselfish, so giving, and 100 percent man, you are my soldier for both the Lord and the US Army, humble and full of the Holy Ghost. A father, friend, fabulous lover, and my hero, you have childlike faith and were completely made for me. It is with great honor that I call you my husband, Mr. Walter Lee Kirkland.

Walter, you came and rescued me from the pit of hell itself. Drinking, cursing, clubbing, adulterous, abused, and on my way to the stripper pole, I heard you speak into my life and let me know that I was supposed to live and not die. Being obedient and assured in God, you told me, "Christy, come out from among them and be made whole." When everyone called me adulterous, you called me anointed. When you were instructed to find a virtuous woman, you never gave up on God changing my life. Never wavering in your walk with Christ but determined to see me live, you took my hand and brought me to my knees and you closed our eyes and introduced me to Jesus Christ.

Ten years later, we are still here on our knees together, praying and interceding for one another and couples all over the world. Honey, for all the nights of staying up praying with me, explaining the word to me, never looking down on my shortcomings, being patient, and allowing God to do a miracle in me, I thank you. Sweetheart, I want you to know I am so much more of a woman today because you took the time to lead me to Jesus Christ. The one, who could fix all those issues you couldn't begin to figure out. In our union and oh, yes, a great sex life, we have three beautiful children: Walter Jr., William Princeton, and Elisabeth Rose Kirkland. Honey, I dedicate this book to you.

Let the Church Say Amen!

Acknowledgments

I acknowledge Jesus Christ as the ultimate Lord of my life and marriage. Thank you for being my personal relationship specialist, restoring my life, and most of all, for saving my life.

To my mother and father, thank you for being obedient and desiring to have me. I love you both.

To my sisters and brothers, I love you Carolyn, Connie, Chris, and Caleb.

To a gifted young lady who helped bring clarity to this book in its infancy stages, Shermaine Nettles.

Most of all, to my own children, Walter, William, and Elisabeth, I love you all for allowing Mommy time to write.

To the focus group couples, thank you for your time, devoted support, and insight. All of your words have helped to shape this book in so many ways.

To my spiritual parents at Faith Mission Ministries Inc., Bishop Harold K. and Prophetess Gwendolyn Browning, this is just the beginning of all you have spoken into my life. By faith, the best is yet to come! Thanks for laying the foundation of faith in my family. You are both the epitome of Christ in all you do and I love you both so much.

WARNING

If you are reading this book, you are in for a blessing in your marriage. I pray that God would show you areas in your marriage in which the enemy has set up shop and that those walls would come down as you pray and read this book. With God, everything that is hidden or done in the dark must be made known in the light. For every place that your feet would tread in your home, I pray it's blessed. I also command the angels of the Lord to be with you through this journey of taking back and having dominion in your marriage.

In every fight there is a causality of war, but by the Spirit of the Lord, it will not affect you or your home. Although you may have been hurt, you can get up; you can love to trust and love again with the strength and help of the Almighty God. Bad memories are not forgotten, but they are mashed into the sea of forgiveness. I pray your bedroom is blessed in Jesus' name. (That the spouse brings you a long-lasting love, that your nights are filled with the sweet aroma of you and him/her, and that your morning brings you smiles.)

You shall love one another not of yourselves and in your ability, but with an understanding and knowledge of each other. I pray that you are strengthened as you begin to fight for your marriage. Know that the Lord has sent His host of heavenly angels before you and the way is being prepared even now. As you are praying for every area in your marriage, believe and have faith that God is working on your behalf. You shall have what you ask for, so get ready for it.

Don't ever forget that "anything worth having for is worth fighting for." Every marriage is not ordained by God and therefore every marriage is not worth fighting for when God has not established it. With every turn of this manual, stop and pray for the power of God to be evident in your marriage. Take the time to perform each activity after the chapter and ask God to help you apply each principle learned to your life. Allow the Spirit of Truth to come in and reveal a better plan, one that demands results and will never depart from you. I pray apart of this book fits into the tailor-made plan of God, that you become fulfilled and truly in love with one another. Now!

The Spirit Realm

"Finally, my brethren, be strong in the Lord, and in the power of his might. Put on the whole armor of God that ye may be able to stand against the wiles of the devil. For you wrestle not against flesh and blood, but against principalities, against powers, against the rulers of the darkness of this world, against spiritual wickedness in high places."
Ephesians 6:10–12

Prologue

The Spirit Realm

> In the spirit realm of life, you must approach everything with wisdom from the Lord and walk in the Spirit.

Lester Sumrall, world-renowned pastor and evangelist, in his book *60 things God Said about Sex,* sheds more light on your spirit and sex:

"You are also a spirit. God created your body and soul; but the God-breathed, eternal essence within you is your spirit. The spirit is the divine element that reminds your soul of God's will for your life. Your soul will be held accountable for the decisions it makes, for the Bible says, 'The soul that sinneth, it shall die' (Ezek. 18:4). The spirit, though, does not die; it returns to God (see Ecclesiastes 12:7). The ecstasy of your spirit, your consciousness of faith in God, and all the other aspects of your spirit are involved in the sex act. Your spirit can employ the sex drive to honor God—if your soul permits it."

Attempting to rely on oneself within a marriage and not fully on the Lord is like sending a toddler to war. He appears big with weapons and gear, but sooner or later the real baby misses his mom. He forgets all his weapons and death is inevitable. As a child in marriage, what seems like all fun and games in the beginning is more serious than you think as time passes by. Just because you know how to have sex does not mean you don't rely on God in this area. Without the help of our Father, wasted opportunities and destruction will take place.

When you have sex, it is a spiritual matter. It is such a matter that a whole book was written, Song of Solomon, and a large majority of the subjects throughout the Holy bible discuss sex in some aspect. Many Christians know this but never pray about sex in their marriages. Nor is it a regular topic you'll hear in the church. I have spoken with numerous Christian couples that believe marriages, including their own, should just thrive or get by with sex. They have never really prayed about sex in the bedroom in such a way as to bring God glory. For many Christian couples, sex is simply just something you do and not an area that requires continuous prayer.

Luke 18:1 instructs us that men ought to always pray and not to faint. Marriage is not complicated, but we can certainly make it so when we walk in the flesh and not in the Spirit. "There is a way which seemeth right unto a man; but the end thereof are the ways of death" (Proverbs 14:12). In marriage, the equation must always remain: God (You + Spouse) and/or (God + You) + (God + Spouse).

In John 15, Jesus declares, "You can do nothing by yourselves, nothing. I am the vine and ye are the branches: He that abideth in me and I in him, the same bringeth forth much fruit: for without me ye can do nothing." *So why are you trying to run your marriage in the flesh?* How long will you keep getting by in your bedroom and never lift your circumstances in that area up to God? When are you going to submit your way of thinking completely over to God, even the so-called good or bad thoughts? Could God be telling you to be softer, take your time, put some perfume on, and rebuke the spirit that tells you not to have sex (great sex) with your spouse? Could the same spirit that commanded Adam and Eve to be fruitful and multiply and walk in the garden buck naked be telling you the same thing? Absolutely! Or could it be your mindset saying, "You don't have to satisfy your spouse; he or she needs deliverance. All she or he wants is sex and more sex; he or she is wrong, so what's spiritual about that?"

Spiritually, sex is the opportunity to come together with your spouse in a way you should share with no one else while here on earth. As spiritual beings dwelling in an body, sex is a luxury to the married that God has given mankind to carry out in His plan. Heaven has no place for sex and for this very reason we are instructed to enjoy one another, while married here on earth. In heaven, God is love and everything we will need and ever desire. Once there, our spirits are one with the ultimate bride, Jesus Christ.

In having sex, you share a sacred place that no one but your spouse should touch or enter into or go out from. Yes, your mom loves you and your father does too, but the Bible declares, "A man is to leave his mother and father and go to cleave unto his wife," and only there can he begin a love that even his parents was never able to give him. That place—your heart, your bedroom—and the coming together as one is an act in which God says, "It is good."

It does not matter how long you have been married or how much you think you have this whole sex area figured out, without the Spirit of God it is only a matter of time before the one you love doesn't love you back. Sex between you and your love is a work in progress, but too many couples don't take the time to work together in this area. Whether in the natural or the spiritual, this act becomes more of a nuisance than a blessing. But God can instruct you in such a way that when you pray prior to making love, you will experience places and groves in your loved one you never knew existed. But if you faint, give up, or throw in the towel in this spiritual matter, it will lead to many problems down the road for the both of you for as long as you dwell together.

The Bible doesn't lie. "Except the Lord build the house, they labor in vain that build it" (Psalm 127:1). God instructs us to walk in the spirit so that you do not fulfill the lust of the flesh. It is flesh that says to abstain from having sex without prayer, put on a long gown, and be mean for no reason; don't be open to talk about sex since there is nothing to talk about; and most of all, it is flesh that tells you there is no need to pray about this area in your life. As long as you continue to have sex and see things in the flesh, you will be out of sync with God every time and cause unnecessary confusion in your bedroom.

The same husband that tells you to put on something sexy is the same man that will help you get a prayer through for your life. The same wife who prays for your favor and is the reason you have favor even now is still anointed when she says no. Don't take the man or woman from his or her anointing when it comes to pleasing one another, but respect that anointing on his or her life when he or she asks you to give what is needed the most. It's the same spirit. But when you walk in the Spirit and abide in Him, you shall ask what you will and it shall be given.

We may be spiritual beings that live in flesh bodies, but we still have needs and wants divinely appointed by God in order to rule our home and survive while here on earth. Your sex drive and your spouse are not from the enemy but from God. Your battle is not with one another but with the principalities—against powers, against rulers of the darkness of the world, against spiritual wickedness in high places—and we are instructed to put on the whole armor of God. Only in the Lord can we be strong enough in His might to stand and protect everything that the enemy sends our way, even in our bedrooms. Pray about what you desire in this area with God and begin to talk with the one you love about how you really feel. Go ahead, ask God to give you a better sex life right now with your loved one, and believe by faith, that you have it.

Walk in the Spirit and give no place to the flesh. Selah.

Now, Let the Church Say Amen!

Introduction

You go to church, you read the Bible, and you pray, but your sex life is just that, a life of its own. You hear "not tonight, I have a headache" so much that you stop praying for your loved one to get better. If it's not a headache it's something else or anything to avoid having *sex*. When you hear those words, you know it means no sex tonight or even this week, maybe. In retaliation of not being able to have sex, you go all out in your thoughts, and what comes out your mouth stings like a viper.

"No concern for me and what I need? Well, I don't have any concern for you and that headache and whatever other problems you might have now!" Two weeks pass and you are ready for sex again. You have tried to build up kudos by cleaning the house, praying, going to church, being nice, and even running the bathwater, then you hear the dreaded words "not to …" You can't even stand to hear the words finish. Emotionally, you just need a release, a release from everything you have coming at you as a man and the best way you feel to do that is to be with your wife right now.

For the woman in need, it's your desire just to lay down tonight with your husband and not want sex, but to cuddle and have him reassure you about how thankful he is for you. This is all you want right now; besides, you just took a bath. She thinks, maybe sex in the morning or even after a good talk tonight before bed. But from the looks of it, neither one of these people will be getting their way.

For the husband, he asks, "What is wrong with you? What is going on in your mind concerning sex? What happened to us? Where is my hot wife? Why is sex a problem for you now when it wasn't at first? Why have the children taken over our bed, and I never see you at your best anymore?" In response to his accusations, the wife responds,

"Well, where is my knight in shining armor? The man who takes care of my mental needs as well as my physical needs, where is he? Where is the man who wanted foreplay all day and then as a result, great sex at night?" For the both of you, the thoughts continue, but no one says anything, another night of frustration and no sex.

Continually, the thoughts take away your joy for one another and as you sleep your mind still speaks for you. "How can this person you married know how to minister to God more than he or she knows how to minister to you? Why, with all the time in church, are you not more of a loving person both spiritually and sexually to me? How about wanting to please me and win me over with what it is I really desire? What happened to our first ministry, being fruitful and multiplying?"

After many sleepless nights, no sex, and no honest communication or real feedback on the issues taking place, you try and ask: "What's happening to us wanting to exercise what comes natural as humans? Why wait to get married just to say not tonight? Why should I hurt so badly every time you make love and never talk about it? Why do we try to make each other mad just to avoid sex? Why is it so hard to tell you how I'm feeling, but when I talk to my friends, I respond better to them? Where's that look you use to have when you wanted me? How is it possible for you to stare at another person and never look twice at me? How did you get this far gone in marriage, that each day waking up beside your spouse is a nightmare? Why are we still married when we have no joy, no fun, and no more sex between us? Why are we even here?"

Sound familiar? Whether it does or doesn't, God has a remedy for these type of silent wars in the bedroom. Having sex is a responsibility, just like your finances, prayer life, children, jobs, and every other part of your marriage that you enlisted to do when you said I do. When you don't have an active sex life that brings the both of you pleasure as married people, you are not living according to the will of the God. "It is God's will for man and woman to be fruitful and multiply and replenish the earth" (Genesis 1:28). Throughout this book, you will learn God's plan for your sex life and why sex is such a vital part of marriage.

Although there are many books on the shelves that deal with sex, many of them have missed the fact that we live on three planes: spirit, soul, and body. Because of our dispositions as saints, we must learn how to walk in the Spirit and be in harmony with our spouses. How you *approach, access,* and *fight* the problems that arise in your sex life as married couples makes all the difference in the spirit realm as well as in the natural world. God ordained the ministry of sex and because of this, like everything that is holy and created by God, it will be attacked. It is written in Matthew 11:12, "The Kingdom of heaven suffers violence and the violent take it by force."

No matter how bad your sex experience is at this time, you can receive freedom and balance for this area in your life. You can begin to love again. If you are willing, then this book was written with you in mind. One of the greatest statements ever spoken of and the one that must be adopted by married couples is *"anything* worth having is worth fighting for."

What's in Store for You inside this Book?

1. You will learn about the spirit realm that we are instructed to live in and how it affects the sex in your marriage.
2. You will become aware of the core reasons why most marriages have conflict regarding sex.
3. You will explore several misconceptions about sex that Christians in the church believe, but shouldn't.
4. As married couples in the body of Christ, you will be able to *enjoy sex again,* the way the Lord ordained it to be in your relationship.

You will have a better sex life after reading and applying the tactics discussed in this book. I believe God is already preparing a better sex life for you and your spouse, one that's worth having and fighting for!

Sex: Let the Church Say Amen!

Chapter One

Sex is Powerful

Sex is a powerful weapon. Selah. Babies are born from this act, but in the same act, children are molested. Women are raped, but a husband celebrates the breaking of the matrix for the first time on marriage night. On TV you see women showing everything and men holding back nothing. Nowadays, clergymen are not able to fulfill their role as husbands or shepherds, leaving this subject unspoken. Confused, they tell you what you can and cannot do, but none of this came from the Lord. Can you see how this world has sent such a bad picture of what sex is supposed to be and how this same sad picture has crept right into churches all over the globe? Once a pastor or saint of God stands in the pews and says the secret word, *sex,* it's, "Oh, My Gosh! Did he go there?" No wonder you can't share this topic with wholesome talk.

When you hear *sex* in the body of Christ, it is often misunderstood and underestimated. A lot of times, pastors may desire to speak on this subject, but the enemy quickly shuts them down due to their own lack of understanding and deliverance in this area. But no matter how you see sex, let me paint this picture in your mind: *sex is a powerful weapon.* When you think about a weapon, two things come to mind: a device designed to injure and kill or something used to gain advantage. It is so complex a topic that many prelates and church members shy away from the subject all together. How can you possibly talk about sex in the same line with Christ in the church? Let me ask you something: will you come out of the closet and just say there is still a lot to be learned about this powerful weapon?

This three-letter word seems to fall in the unwholesome conversation category instead of your common Tuesday night Bible study category. Even among the adults it's not appropriate to discuss prayer for this area in your marriage. You can pray about migraines, infidelity, and just about anything else, but walk in church one day and ask your pastor to pray for your sex life. Pray that the sex in your life becomes a weapon to defeat every devil that comes against your bedroom and what God has ordained for you and your spouse.

This is what a lot of people in the body of Christ fail to realize: in the same sense that sex can kill, sex is the way God creates life. What other weapon can you think of that can kill and injure and then turn around and bring you and God glory? It's really hard when you look at it that way, but it is the truth; no other weapon has had so many effects on people as this one. Let's look at this weapon over time and today.

1. Sex, unlike guns and drugs, has been around since God created man and woman. This weapon is powerful. It is the one thing that has not ceased to exist.
2. 1 Corinthians 7:5 says, "Defraud ye not one the other, except it be with consent for a time." This Scripture instructs you as a married couple to talk about periods of not having sex or it can turn around and injure you both.
3. Going without sex for a long time without the help of the Lord can cause one to react to self, others, and life differently (masturbation, selfishness, frustration, adultery, celibacy problems, and more).
4. People have had their virginity taken and it has since scarred their total outlook on the sex act. Or, they have left what was natural for them as man and woman to be received by the same sex.
5. People have cheated on their loved ones for instant gratification that, at home, was never instant. The affair happened and the marriage died. Do I really need to go on?

Sex has the ability to have life changing effects on people, both good and bad. There are a lot of married people today that, because of the scars of sex in their past, cannot and will not have sex again even though they are married. When they do, the power of the past that has overtaken them causes them to go back to that sex scene all the time. Instead of people actually enjoying their sex lives, resentment and lack of understanding shows up every time and annihilates the very thought of being together. In other words, you just keep putting off the reality that you both need healing in this area. But once again, since it's sex, one person sees it as something they can live without, while the other person simply cannot. Joyce Meyers said, "Anything you refuse to deal with has power over you. Many people never experience peace or joy because of unresolved issues in their lives."

God has promised us through His Word that we have everything that pertains to life and godliness and that without Him we can do nothing. Why do so many couples refuse to take up this matter with the very God of the universe who created them and who says daily, "Come now and let us reason together" (Isaiah 1:15)? God wants to take away your burdens and show you how to be a wife or a husband to one another. He can show a wife how to say yes to her husband when he asks for sex, and then turn around and show a husband how to hold his wife when she craves intimacy in the way only he can give.

God is able to carry every problem you as a saint wrestle with on Himself and give you such peace of mind when dealing with your loved one in this area. There is absolutely nothing too hard for our Lord and Savior, Jesus Christ. The very problems that you refuse to deal with that keep tearing down the walls in your marriage can be restored and built up for the both of you, but only by God.

But without the Spirit of God, what you say you will never do causes you to eat the very words you once said with one simple act: sex. We need the power of God to show us where we really are as couples. So you pray and fast, but deep down inside of mankind is the emotional bank that stays as hot as volcano called a sex drive. When it's not being released, it has the tendency to blow, and when it does, things can happen that not even mankind desires to talk about.

Women are so unique in that we need God to show us how to be in harmony with our bodies and our husbands' bodies so we are able to meet their needs with a willing heart and not a "just do it to get it over with" attitude. "What I want to do, that I do not do, but that which I do not want to do, I do" (Romans 3:23). Sex is so powerful, but even in this statement things exist which can leave both the male and female scarred for life for one main reason: when sex is not a consensual act between two people, emotionally the male and female can become damaged and the reality of healing can seem so far away. You don't have to look to the world to see how sex can become a weapon, because the Bible has plenty of examples to look at.

1. In the book of Judges, Samson had an uncontrollable appetite for women, such an appetite that it lead to the Philistine army coming in and cutting away his glory (hair) and removing the weapon of God from him for a season (Judges 16).
2. The wisest man that ever lived, Solomon, was unwise in his dealings with this powerful weapon of sex, and so was his dad. His overindulgent life with women eventually led to the destruction of his kingdom. Solomon had over 700 wives and 300 concubines, and eventually his wives turned away his heart (1 Kings 11:3).
3. David's son, Amnon, raped his own sister, Tamar, because of her beauty and his uncontrollable desire to have sex. Then afterward he hated her (2 Samuel 13:14).
4. David also allowed self-indulgence in this weapon to get the best of him and, therefore, he lost a son as a result of having Uriah killed to lie with his wife, Bathsheba (2 Samuel 11).
5. The men of the city, even the men of Sodom, wanted the angels that came to visit Lot to come out that they might know them (Genesis 19:5).

Amnon and Solomon were young men and, like their father, they failed in this area. Were these men not talked to about sex since their father really struggled in this area himself? Were David and Bathsheba embarrassed or afraid to speak to these boys about their sex life ahead of them? Who taught them about this weapon and how it, if not used right, has the potential to kill? In some foreign countries, little boys are taught at an early age how to be soldiers of war. They carry guns that even our own military would not dream of allowing young children to carry. Well, take that same picture and put sex in the hands of the immature, evil, and self-indulgent at heart, walking in the flesh, and you will see why sex can be so powerful.

Very rarely are young girls these days being taught the beauty of waiting for the man who is willing to wait for her. They are raised to find someone to take care of them and if it looks saved, it must be saved. I just wonder if trying the Spirit is

> **While mentioning the youth, let's take a quick look at our youth today regarding sex.**

even mentioned or taught to young girls in the body of Christ. Instead, as saints, you tell the young ladies how to supposedly pick a suitor. Prime candidates are the preacher's son or the student in class who seems to have himself together. If he sounds saved and quotes a few Scriptures, he has good potential. Making sure he has a real walk with Christ and a convicting relationship with God is the last thing on their little minds. Choosing a young man that has respect for himself and a young lady is not preached enough to our youth in churches.

Who is teaching our young girls about the power of sex and its grip over your life once it has taken place? Are you honestly too embarrassed to prepare and equip our young girls for the road of sex ahead? Who are the mothers and fathers that will tell their daughters the truth about how it hurts, heals, and can turn around and be a complete mystery, even in your own marriage? Sex is powerful! Do you really want your daughter or son walking around with a loaded pistol ready to whip it out on everyone? Are you taking the time to train, mold, and make sure your daughter fully understands what it is that the Lord has blessed her with? Unless the young man is a blessing and ready to receive her as wife, bless no one. Amen.

Young men are not exempt either. Nowadays, if young men are in the church and they are sexually active, it's accepted as long as it's on the down, down low. They are in church all day and have no power over what they feel between their legs. As the preacher preaches, sex is all over their little minds. As parents, you may have the tendency to be so focused on getting your own sex life together that you become ignorant of the inner wars taking place in your little man's life. Frustrated and scared to address the fact that the timing of understanding sex in your child's life is upon you, you push the talk to the side or ignore him altogether. You don't take the time to talk with him about what he is feeling: what is normal, not normal, the truth, and the lies.

Most of all, you don't even feel an unction from the Lord telling you to explain to your children what you experienced from with this powerful weapon. It is going to hurt to share with your children what you went through so they don't go that way, so instead you just feel led to tell them to go and pray. Their best witness to the truth and the unadulterated understanding of sex you have just kept from them. Now they will never come back to you to talk about this act. Instead, they will continue to seek truth elsewhere, however it's given, as long as some of their questions get answered. Even if they don't ask, don't wait to explain this great mystery that God has instructed us as parents to explain to our youth today. Your own testimony about how you have experienced sex is more powerful than you think, especially when you ask God to guide your conversation.

But whatever you do, don't allow your shortcomings to rob your children of a chance to understand one of the most powerful acts of living in the whole world. If you are hearing about sex and seeing the signs of sexual postures and lust on parade, go to God and pray. Ask Him to direct your tone and your message to reach your children. Don't become judgmental, but remember what no one ever told you; you can now be saving the very life of your child. What if someone could have explained it better to you; how would you be? Allow it to be you this time and save your children from experiencing sex in a way that you wish could have been different for you.

You pray about your feelings and shortcomings in the bedroom, but you never pray about the many sensitivities and sexual desires in your children.

Start today because before you know it, the season of unquenched lust will be tapping at the door of your young girl or boy. If your children's season is already here, that's okay, too. I'm just glad you know. But go ahead and begin to pray and ask God to lead your conversation regarding your children and sex. But please realize that you have to talk to them about how powerful this act is.

For single moms in the church, they may know their boys are having sex and say nothing. Why? They are dealing with so much with their own sex lives, trying to keep the man they are not married to, what can they possibly say to their sons? Every time a single mother wants to sow a seed into the young man's life, the enemy quickly comes and says, "You aren't married; what can you say? You are still dealing with not having enough yourself and a man who only really wants you for your body."

A large majority of single mothers today are becoming too embarrassed to talk openly about their own sexual desires to get help from anyone spiritual. Some single disobedient and bold women keep the boyfriend on the side and walk up prideful in the church. All the while, her son is watching every step and move she makes. Satan whispers, "What are you going to say? You shack up, why can't he? After all, you planted the seed and look where the roots ran to." In front of her son, the picture he sees of her is tainted and she knows it is. What can you possibly tell him about sex? Her excuse when he begins to have sex is, "He has no father figure." Well speak the truth, sister: he has no mother, either. If he did, he would have a better godly example living in front of him and pointing into the right direction despite what his single mom may have to endure. *Let the church say amen.*

Married couples who struggle with sex themselves may find it challenging to have an honest talk with their son. As the young man begins to express how he truly feels about sex to his parents, his openness turns into a debate between them or a religious argument about his lustful motive to have sex. As the man speaks, the woman turns to say, "What can you tell him when you and I aren't even having sex? You are the one that is so glad your son has finally gotten to this point. Now you can relate to him instead of making sure he doesn't go down the path you chose." Mothers, can also get in the way by supporting unhealthy relationship as long as the young lady is somewhat calmly.

If couples are struggling, a quick fix or maybe to help play down his sexual craving, he is told to put his flesh under subjection, but never taught how to do this. If talking to your child about sex is too sensitive to you because of the disagreement between you and your spouse, seek God earnestly for guidance or get professional help. Don't allow your quandary to be an excuse for your child's sin. As long as the both of you are not in agreement in this area or you do not support one another on the counsel that is given, the child will struggle, unless he has someone sober to talk to. Because coming into manhood is so life changing, if a young man is not able to find and trust in the words of those he speaks to concerning this manner, he will probably never come to you again.

Sex, is going to happen, whether you want it to or not, it's just a matter of when and where.

Now if you and your spouse are walking together in oneness, this is all the more reason to speak with your children about the issue, but don't be so detached from your children that you can't see when your son or daughter really needs to be talked to candidly about his body and her prized possession. Just remember: holy or not, if you don't tell him the truth and pray as you talk, he will learn it on his own. So, what does Satan say to married couples who aren't walking in oneness? How can you talk about something you aren't even doing? You can't even please your own spouse. As Christians, we are to study to show ourselves approved unto God concerning the trials we go through. Even our children need to be ready in season and out of season for trials that will come their way.

Lies are all over this world, but there is a problem when deceit begins to creep into the church. As the body of Christ, we have accepted a lot of these lies about sex due to the lack of teaching on what is and isn't acceptable that has gone forth. Just because sex is not taught at church and the fact that you may have setbacks in your own relationship does not negate the need for young men and women to know that sex is powerful and in the wrong hands can cause serious injury. If they are asking, you better start talking and asking God to direct your conversation toward them.

If you desire to help your child grow, then instruct them on just how powerful sex can be as a weapon. Don't allow your setback to become your son's or daughter's shortcomings. No matter how you receive it, married, single, or whatever, sex is a weapon. Sex is to marriage as the blood of Jesus is to salvation. When you go without understanding on these subjects, you will have something you have no clue how to operate, but is yet so powerful.

In the unlearned, sex can be detrimental. Knowing how to speak about sex to young children and the one you love, is very important. Talking about sex with anyone is a process itself, but if said the wrong way or not said at all it can cause injury to your child today and forever. Set the example; start educating yourself early about your teenager and the problems they have to deal with. Do your homework on where your children are prior to talking to them about sex. Begin praying ahead for their sexual activity and for the desire to wait until they are married to be a part of their makeup. Don't set your children up to walk down the same road that you traveled.

If you really love the generation you are raising, lead and guide them into the truth. Help them to depend on the Holy Spirit to lead them down the road that has been predestined for them. As you speak, they will be receptive and you can trust that the words you speak, God's Spirit, will keep them in perfect peace.

Declare today, in Jesus name, that your children can and will wait for sex and that they will have an understanding of how powerful this act is in their lives after you have spoken life to them concerning this situation. That, in due season, they shall reap if they faint not, and because of your desire for them to live and God in them, that no weapon, thought, or imagination formed against them shall entangle them by any means. They shall know the truth and the truth shall make them free. Amen.

Sex Can Injure You and Your Spouse:

Adultery can be forgiven, and cheating doesn't just happen overnight. If you want to learn something about these two topics, you don't have to go far because the Holy Bible is full of these types of extramarital affairs. Jesus Christ, our Lord and Savior, is well acquainted with every situation when it comes to sex, both the good and bad. Whether the Bible talks about your specific hurt or not, Jesus understands everything in the area of sex. All over the Old and New Testaments, we hear of spiritual adultery, prostitution, sex slaves, orgies, lust, pornography, incest, and other unimaginable things. So, when someone has an affair or cheats, we need to remember that we serve a God who in all points was tempted but was without sin; a God who understands our temptations very well and therefore begs for us to come to Him so we may be made whole when we fall short.

On the injured end, it is only through God that you are able to forgive, but never become a slave to the memory. God has the ability to help you renew your mind and also change the perspective for the one that cheats. Do you think He doesn't understand? He does. The very world He gave His life for has turned its back on Him for other gods: money, lust, fame, and just about anything else you can imagine. Despite all of our shortcomings and adulterous ways, God is still offering a seat in heaven and a chance for everyone to enjoy the benefits of serving Him. Of course it's hard for you to see (but detrimental to Christ) how someone you love can go outside the bounds of trust. Sometimes it's just outright devastating, but think of all the people who cheat on God and then go back to Him every time asking the Lord to please forgive them. Now please don't think cheating or committing adultery is an excuse to sin because it isn't. Each time we sin, we crucify the Lord all over again. He died on the cross so that all our sins would be forgiven, now and the ones to come.

If anybody understands hurt and pain, it's God and because of that, He is able to bear up all our pain. When injured, we are instructed by God to cast all our burdens on Him and allow Him to care for us while the healing takes place. Whenever an injury occurs, healing takes time, especially in the area of sex because it involves so many dimensions of a human being. Spiritually, you sin against God; physically, you sin against your body, as well as the one you love; and in the soul, you engage in an almost never ending battle for your mind, will, and emotions.

Isaiah 1:18–19 declares, "Come now, let us reason together, though your sins are as scarlet, they shall be white as snow; though they are red like crimson, they shall be as wool. If ye be willing and obedient, ye shall eat the good of the land." So when you forgive your loved one for going beyond the bounds of your commitment, trust that we have a God who admonishes you to take on His forgiveness, and only through His strength and His leadings can He revive your hearts again. He can help you heal everywhere you hurt. When sex is taken away and the desire goes out the door, he can renew this area in your life, too. He created the sex drive in the first place, and if He can give a man sight, He can give you exactly what you are asking for in your sex life. You just have to ask for this area to be made whole again and receive your total healing.

A lot of people in church forgive but refuse to forget. They no longer do the things they used to do as couples, nor do they let the other person forget they cheated, but they stay married and miserable. They even go so far as to keep living in the same house, but never show love to the other person for fear of what others would say if they were divorced. Well, I say if you live like this, you are already divorced and this is not living, but bondage according to God. This is living with the mouth and not with your heart. You said you had forgiven, but your actions tell another story. This will not only affect your spouse, but your children, too.

When you forgive with your mouth only, you allow yourself to become more entrapped than the one who committed the actual act. This is a sign of forgiving in your own ability, but when you operate in the ability of God, you not only forgive, but you also restore that person. "Brethren, if a man be overtaken in a fault, ye which are spiritual, restore such a one in the spirit of meekness; considering thyself, lest thou also be tempted" (Galatians 6:1). When a person violates the marriage vows, the sin has to be handled delicately. Even though you are hurt and seem to not be able to put the act behind you, when you are in the place of restoring the one who has sinned, you have to be watchful over your own life as the thoughts, accusations, dreams, and emotions will come to bombard your vision of the one you love. In all your spiritual might, it is possible to be brought down to your absolute lowest while dealing with the sin of your loved one.

Now, I said all of that to come to this conclusion about adultery. Matthew 6:31–32 tells us, "It has been said, Whosoever shall put away his wife, let him give her a writing of divorcement. But I say unto you, That whosoever shall put away his wife, saying for the cause of fornication, causeth her to commit fornication, causeth her to commit adultery; and whosoever shall marry her that is divorced committeth adultery." The only exception given by Jesus Christ himself is for the cause of fornication, or sexual unfaithfulness. Based on this Scripture, adultery or fornication is legitimate grounds for divorce. On the flipside, Scripture never commands that anyone "must" divorce an unfaithful spouse.

Although the pain and hurt are clearly in front of you, the forgiving spouse must remember we still have sinful natures and are in need of a Savior, and that's why Jesus Christ died. In each child of God dwells no good things and we are told to die daily. We would like to assume we are made perfect and we are in His Spirit, but we must never forget that every man or woman still suffers with dying to the old man. Romans 7:23-24 declares, "But I see another law in my members, warring against the law of my mind, and bringing me into captivity to the law of sin which is in my members. O wretched man that I am! who will deliver me from this body of death?"

Out of the same mouth we say I love you with, our hearts still bleed with our old nature. But, "I the Lord search the heart, *I* try the reins, even to give every man according to his ways, *and* according to the fruit of his doings" "The heart *is* deceitful above all *things,* and desperately wicked: who can know it?" (Jeremiah 17:9-10). Our hearts, although we say we have given them, are the very things God says are desperately wicked above all and that no one can know but Him. It is imperative that we stay connected to God so that he can reveal to us our shortcomings—what's really going on inside of us—and only then can we not fall victim to the enemy in this area. We are living in the disposition of grace because of Jesus Christ and the power of His blood. It is only by grace that we can be saved from the torment of hell, and it is only by the grace of God that a person filled with the spirit of God can forgive the one who commits an act of adultery. What was once a sin—and yes, adultery still is—God forgives. Before you throw in the towel and write off something God has put together, take this case to the feet of Jesus, allow Him to heal your heart, and allow Him to help the one who has cheated.

Forgiveness is never easy to accept no matter what form it comes in because it involves so much breaking of the human soul. The mind, will, and even emotions have to surrender to will of the Spirit. Before receiving the Lord into my life, I was married to a man who chose to live his life and make decisions without regard to our commitment. As a result, and being a heathen myself, I did the same. We both were living outside our marriage vows to one another. Once I received the Lord in my life, it was time to quit all this lascivious living, but my husband at the time did not want that life and therefore granted my request for divorce.

Today I am happily married to a man who loves the Lord and who knows how to treat me and our family well. We have three beautiful children, and yes, the fruit of my womb is blessed and not cursed. He is a man who prays, fasts, and devotes his morning together with me to cover our home and our vision. He has been blessed almost every year of his life to receive a promotion from the army, and I would like to just interject this point for all religious-minded people. God reigns on whoever He wills. What He allows for one person is His grace and mercy, not what any man thinks or believes is best for the person. When man said I was cursed, God caused me to be blessed. When I thought I would never know anything about love, he introduced me to Love itself, Jesus Christ. And in finding Christ, He allowed the love of my life to find me. After all the hurt and shame of being married before, I was restored and able to love again.

In spite of several people who called me sinful and said marrying me would only be against the will of God since I had been divorced, Walter heard from the Lord himself and asked me to marry him. Was I the best image of a saint at the time? No, but I was on my way to knowing all I could about Christ and what love was really about.

I was chasing Jesus; He was preparing me and, all the while, the Lord was sending me a man to show me how to love again. I know the leaders at the church meant well at the time by instructing Walter to find a so-called virtuous woman, one already filled with the Holy Ghost, maybe a choir member. But I thank God for Walter, who already had a personal relationship enough with God to trust His leading, asking for my hand in marriage. To this day, he is not only an inspiration to me, but a constant reminder that Christian leaders are to be a light, showing and teaching us the way, but it is ultimately God who is to be our guide.

When it comes to being a leader, it can be very easy to interject your advice or opinions concerning what someone should do or not do when extreme situations take place. Why? Because so many church members today are expecting you to tell them what to do instead of them hearing from God themselves. You teach them on a weekly basis, but it's not enough; they want you to almost do it for them. Nobody wants to wait; even in the body of Christ we want microwave results with overnight answers. But I thank God for leaders who are in tune with the Spirit of God, continuing to usher couples into His presence and teaching them how to wait to hear from God. Does it hurt? Yes. Is it a process? Definitely. Will it work? Absolutely. Christian leaders who have your best interest at heart and chase after God know that even though they offer guidance, it will ultimately be God that brings change to your lives. These are the leaders who don't want you to become handicapped by their feeding, but desire you to taste and see that the Lord is good and His mercy endures forever.

What is a handicapped Christian? It is a Christian who receives counsel from the pastor, feels bound to stick with what the pastor has asked them to do (because of their lack of spiritual growth), and never prays to see that the word they have heard from the pastor lines up with what God is speaking to their hearts.

Since a couple is hurting and not able to wait, pray themselves, and hear from God, whatever the pastor says goes, even if it means living with someone you make yourself love forever. The act has never let you forget and for years you can never move forward. Every day you pray for what the pastor says and with your heart you wish the other person who cheated was dead or would just leave. Even if he or she stays, the pain is sometimes so unbearable you don't even pray. Make no mistake about it now, pastors are there to be direct when you cannot make sound decisions on your own in extreme cases, but never to replace your own personal relationship with Jesus Christ and your ability to hear God for yourself in regard to His instructions for you. Not only will God give you the answer to your dilemma, He will be responsible for everything it entails for you and your loved one.

Pastors who are aware of the danger of becoming the god-figure in a person's life are after the heart of God and have that person's best interests in mind. They have their own healthy and effective marriages and therefore can give you sound counsel in line with what God desires for you. This type of leader, when it comes to marital counseling, is aware that, although they have not walked a mile in the shoes of Jesus, they are not God, they cannot give grace to any man, and in spite of the situation, they understand the couple has to come to final decisions within themselves after sound doctrine, counsel, and prayer together.

Once a person has been injured by sex and vows are violated, it is the responsibility of both partners to make sure they lay at the feet of Jesus so he can heal the couple inside and out. Like a health inspector, God judges their hearts, joints, marrows, and intentions. By doing this, God is glorified in their lives and actions as they govern themselves in their house. The decision they make will be what they are held accountable for by God and not man.

Many times, the injury has to do with both sides of our behavior. It's not so much what a person has done to sin, but what they have not done in marriage that has provoked the other to sin. Lack of things like love, listening, attention, self-awareness, respect, appreciation, and most of all, sex, or having boring or just horrible sex can lead to adultery among other things. In churches all over the world, couples hide their true emotions toward one another and even the priest in an effort to hide the real wars that are taking place inside of them. Most of the time, it's sex and they don't know how to just come out and say that is what's really going on; whether it's not enough, none at all, or what each other desires it to be. But God continues to judge the heart and demands the person look inwardly during the process of healing.

He instructs us that there is nothing that He can't see or understand. So, if you can't talk to your pastor and maybe your partner doesn't understand your need for sex, we have a Father who made your male and female organs and if He can turn the hearts of kings, surely he can turn a muscle or desire here or there.

A lot of hurt has to do with not only the person who committed the sin or lacked in something, but the one forgiving the sin. Remember the story of the woman who was caught in the act of adultery? God forgave her when, according to the Laws of Moses, she should have been stoned. But when Jesus asked who was not guilty, no one stayed. At times, Christians become involved in sin and that situation has to be carefully and softly dealt with. When Jesus forgave this woman of the night, she came back and anointed his feet. Who you say no to now, may be the very one you need later. Being led by the Lord, as well as who you allow to counsel you during this very important matter, is the only way to understand and know the will of God for your life after an extramarital affair.

My heart was right and my purpose for getting a divorce was not out of a selfish spirit. It was a personal decision I made with the God of my life, Jesus Christ, and if it was not His will, there is no way I would even be here ministering to anyone. But because of his grace and mercy, I operate in a power in which marriages are being restored and rededicated to Jesus Christ. Proverbs 14:12: "There is a way which seemeth right unto man but the end thereof are the ways of death." I implore you to make sure your ways—your decisions about your acts and your stand on adultery when you forgive—are of the Lord. When you say you forgive, forgive; and move on with a pure heart and never hold the ones you love captive by not releasing them to be free!

Self-Inflicted Injuries

When we put our guards down, the enemy comes in like a flood, setting up shop in the hidden pressure points of our lives. The enemy knows what you lack and moves hastily to offer that to you. Although we are instructed to walk in the Spirit, sometimes we simply just miss it. Satan is neither dumb nor wise, but he thinks he has you and I figured out. The trials he sends are custom-made trials that come to you to get you to sin against God. But one thing you have to know is that you are not alone. Many other Christians have been here before, regardless of what it is, sexual or not. "There hath no temptation taken you but such as is common to man: but God is faithful who will not suffer you to be tempted above that ye are able; but will with the temptation also make a way to escape, that ye may be able to bear it" (1 Corinthians 10:13).

Temptations come in all shapes and sizes to entice us all. So you say you don't deal with lust, but maybe it's gossip or gluttony. Whatever it is, when you are not aware of yourself, even as a Christian, you are capable of falling, but God can come and restore you. He did it for David, Abraham, and others, but most of all, He did it for me. It wasn't too long ago that I ended my long affair with the god of my belly. God has since forgiven and restored me in this area. After a ten-day fast of nothing but water, I lost twenty pounds and received a new way of eating altogether. Every day was a struggle without food, but it showed me just how much I was allowing the god of my belly to run my life. The images, thoughts, and suggestions of eating and sneaking food were endless. Can you believe a grown woman sneaking around to go eat at night in her own house? It made me realize just how little control I had in this area. I now refuse to ever cheat on the Lord in this area again.

My mind is restored and I am so happy to have a new outlook on eating and allowing God to be in total control of my food, thanks to Dr. C. S. Lovett's book, *Help Lord ... The Devil Wants Me Fat!* Of course it is a process, but I am not allowing my belly to dictate anymore what I should eat or drink. Did it hurt knowing I had cheated on the Lord? Of course, and I was determined to earn his trust and allow him to rule my belly. After finding out I was cheating on God with another god, it really hurt me spiritually as well as naturally. How could something as unimportant as food have so much power over me? My eating was literally trying to kill me. (What I thought about food all of my life seemed harmless until God showed me another god in me.) But even in our spiritual affairs, He still takes us back again, over and over, making sure to teach us about the areas we are wrong in. So, let's look at how this affects many of our love lives today.

Like I said, I thought all the food that I made was good and knew what I ate was not always the best, but it was pleasing. Pleasing my flesh. We are all in the body of Christ, but we are far from putting on the heavenly bodies with no sin. This leaves us very susceptible to hidden sins and hidden affairs against our God that in time could very well injure our marriages. When you have lived life for yourself for so long and God tells you that you are a new creature in Christ—behold old things are passed away and new things have come forth—we still have a price to pay for owning this new makeover, and it is simply obedience to God's Word in every area of our lives. The enemy has not forgotten one nasty thing that each of us has done prior to receiving the Lord in our lives.

His way of getting back at us is through our minds. In that powerful brain holds short- and long-term memories, good and bad. Just like a brain, Satan has demonic angels who keep record of the way we lived and he plans to use them at any chance he gets. He thinks you have forgotten that your mind belongs to Christ and although his thoughts come in, you have the power to refute them and send them back to the pit of hell. A lot of couples who fall short in this area find themselves subject to old behaviors or wants that are only there as suggestions from the devil. When the Lord makes us free, we are free indeed. As we are being made over, God shows us what is still a part of us that we need to get rid of, not that anything is wrong with our Spirit, but it's the soul that still has to obey the Word of God. The soul consists of the mind, will, and emotions and if it is not given over to the Lord in word and deed, it can ruin us. This is what the devil is after every day. He knows you have the Spirit of God and he doesn't desire that; he wants the soul of an individual.

Every day he is going to send tactics after each weak area of your life, regardless of where you are. This is why the Bible says to be on your guard; be watchful because the devil goes around seeking whom he may destroy. You would like to think that surely in the bedroom you can put down your guard, and you can, only after you have dethroned the strongholds. If not, these injuries can come back to sabotage your marriage. People don't just wake up and cheat; seeds have to be sown first.

The enemy thinks you have forgotten about your old sex life or old way of living since the Christian life is so good. A lot of couples fall victim to this manipulation and find themselves subject to old behaviors or wants that are only there as suggestions from the enemy. It all comes from not being sober-minded and vigilant in watching out for the enemy and his darts of lies.

You are a Christian now; the enemy knows better than to just send a Jezebel because you will recognize her. Instead, he sends the thoughts and suggestions first. Being unlearned and unskilled in the Word, you don't bring those thoughts into the obedience of Christ. As a result, you end up at a hotel, terrified, and later, your pastor corrects you by saying, "I don't know how you could do such a thing to your spouse ..." My only answer to this is that you reaped a harvest on those seeds you did not uproot or kill quickly with the Word.

If you don't understand anything about sex and marriage, you need to understand seedtime and harvest and how the enemy will try and use it against you. Even though it is a principle in the kingdom of heaven, the enemy uses it all the time. The process: one seed from the enemy of what your wife or husband cannot do into the right soil, well-watered (in your mind, there's someone who the enemy says can do so much more), with a little bit of sunlight (grins and raised eyebrows, showing interest in you) and a harvest comes your way, whether you want it or not. Whatsoever you sow, you will reap, good or bad.

Satan whispers: "You planted the garden, why not eat from it? Of course God will forgive you. Your wife will never do you like this/your husband will never feel like that. Remember, you're used to it this way and your wife would never dream of doing this, go ahead." Or maybe you are in a relationship with an unsaved man who knows nothing about how to be nice or how to pray. "But this deacon is the complete opposite and he can pray, too. Super smooth, even his cologne has a 'drop your panties at the door' smell."

In your mind, you begin to think, "My God! He's single and looking. I need a way out of my marriage anyway, could this be my blessing in disguise?" Satan sends more ideas and suggestions: "Go ahead, your husband isn't saved anyway; how can this be worse than lying?"

Sound familiar? That's because it's the same devil. It's been working for him since the days of Adam and Eve; why stop now?

But thank God for the mind of Christ and the power to speak those things which are not as though they are. When the enemy comes in to attack us as saints, it's always a weak spot he is after. He is so cowardly he will never face us head on; nope, he waits for us to create the opportunity for him to offer his own agenda into our lives. Yes, this man is supposedly everything you don't have, but whatever happened to living by faith, taking your man shopping for the "drop your panties" smell? When was the last time you sat down and told your husband what was pleasing to you and what was not?

Some of the best marriages to date are the ones that have taken the time to speak over one another and in waiting continue to help shape and mold one another. These couples are offering suggestions, praying specifically for the need to be filled in each other's lives, becoming broken before God, and realizing the power of oneness in marriage. They walk in the ability to go to God naked and unashamed, praying that the hand of God would be on the man of God in their home. The wives in these couples are not willing to throw in the towel because their husbands are lacking right now, but continue to confess that in God this man is more than capable of being all he is called to be. I personally refuse to have sown all my prayers and time into a man to simply give up on God. He is able and I shall wait and see the salvation of the Lord come forth in my husband, no matter where he is. I understand that I have what I say, and I say, "My husband lacks in nothing."

I have experienced many of these tests, being away from my husband during his deployments with the army and even right at home. Before this wonderful man I am married to now, I was sexually involved with a lot of men. I am not proud to admit this, but I'm no longer ashamed. That was my life before Christ, amen. I did whatever and went out of my way to please men; however, I felt very nasty when I got married due to this. By then I had already received the Lord in my life, but the suggestions, the ideas, the pictures, and my past lay at the door. Every now and then, like a broken record they played over and over in my mind.

Now look at the devil and his tainted memories of me. Prepared to launch, the enemy thought he had me figured out and he planned his attack very carefully. He knew I liked sex and that I had a lot of men to help carry out this act in the past, because during that time I had a nasty way of thinking about sex. But once I received the Lord in my life, the devil thought that way of thinking would stay a part of me; of course he tried his hardest to get me to adopt this way of thinking as my own, but thank God for the Blood. One night, I asked my husband to get in a certain position and up to that point, I had never told him about my acts of sex. When he did, my mind said another man's name and in an instant I saw that man and me doing what I was now asking my husband to do.

Right in the middle of sex, I had to stop. How in the world can I be in a relationship with the Lord, in a monogamous relationship with my husband, and think about some other man and what we did years ago? But that act had a connection to it; it wanted to wake up something, and the father of lies was there to try and see it through. I told my husband everything, and he began to pray for my mind. Of course, at the time, it wasn't the ideal situation, but I told him what I had seen and he began praying.

A lot of times we are so spiritual we miss the tactics of the devil who come to sabotage our own freedom in the bedroom. Who would ever think Satan would send an arrow in the middle of sex? Right in the middle of sex I am asking my husband to pray. It sounds uncommon, but wake up! The devil has no time limit on his tactics. The enemy hates our guts as married couples and there is no more perfect time for his bowl of tricks. Anytime he catches us unaware of who we are and what the Lord has completely delivered us from, he pounces. What the devil wanted to do was not only bring a picture, but he wanted me to go ahead and do what people who don't value their sex life and their spouses do. He wanted me to accept this as a part of my way of thinking. Maybe I did listen to the enemy's lie before, and from what I could see, no one died, but it was my way of thinking and not God's.

If I would've accepted that seed, that one seed would've grown into another seed. I could've kept going and acted as if I didn't just have the out of body experience and hide this from my husband. But God has given us the power to enjoy the bedroom and not allow anything to defile it. No imaginations, wants, false fantasies, and definitely not my past would take precedence of this new way of thinking that I have in Christ. I understand that in my flesh dwells no good thing and as much as we are instructed to enjoy sex and our flesh, we have to be on our guard, not bringing in our old way of operating. Even in the most heated moments of passion, you still need to be on guard for the enemy and his tactics.

Just so the devil would get no victory, we have since enjoyed that position and when we go there, my honey asks, "Baby, are you okay?" I gladly respond each time by saying, "Yes, *Walter*." It has taken a while, of course, but I don't struggle in that area anymore. I have never forgotten, and I make sure each day that I am mindful of the enemy in my own life and especially my past sexual desires. Everything God does that has a process attached to it is for both you and somebody else. In this case, regarding self-inflicted injuries, it wasn't about my spouse, but about me and how my reactions flowed over to my husband.

I had to learn how to successfully go through the process of dealing with my sexual desires and weakness, all the while learning to not allow my situation to bleed onto my husband. I needed to trust him in knowing where I was as his wife and in doing this, he was free to help me in any way he could. This was not the time to be embarrassed or feel as if he would never understand. It wasn't even fair if I decided to hide this from him because each time I was with him I was paralyzed with this past life. I realized that by bringing my spouse in with me regarding this trial, we both can receive what God has for us. What the enemy meant for bad, God turned around and worked for our good.

I could've kept all this drama to myself and tried to deal with all of these issues, but God wanted to heal me and allow my husband to be able to enjoy me each time and not have to deal with past issues showing up. Couples must be able to understand that many times when the Lord brings you to a place of openness and shows you where you are still in need, this is not the time to go psycho on your spouse. Instead, allow them to understand what you are going through and don't take the blows all by yourself. Trust the growth in your spouse and understand that you both are there for each other. Learning to trust your spouse is a continual process, not an overnight happening.

My husband has since been able to talk to me more openly about what all is going on in my head when we have sex: some bad experiences which held me in bondage for years and thoughts or imaginations that still lay dormant when we are together. It is now his desire without me even asking to help, but this was a process as I opened up more and more with him in the course of our marriage and our conversation has become so open about both our pasts. We are in this sexual act of lovemaking together 100 percent and if I can't give him my all, he is able to without question recognize when I am emotionally absent from him during sex. Because he loves me and knows that sex is what makes him feel wonderful and the same for me, it is important for him to help me make sure I am free when we are together in this way. Self-inflicted or not, don't allow the enemy to rob you both of the pleasure you are to bring to one other.

Sex was never meant to be a one-sided event, but an act created for two people in love and married. Not only married, but wanting the very thing that makes them one to be rekindled all the days of their lives. Be careful, be delicate, be mindful, but most of all, realize self has to die, just like any part of our being, in order for us to be more like Christ. Learn to heal together and trust the God on the inside of both of you. *What glory can God get out of you being delivered alone in something that is meant for the both of you? Let the church say amen.*

PRACTICE IT:

Here are some discussion-starters that can help you begin your journey of healing and prevent injuries from happening in your bedroom.

1. Pray and ask God to show you what areas of your sex life you are still ashamed of or are hiding from your spouse.
2. After praying, talk to your loved one about your wants and needs so that you will not feel like you are fighting against Satan alone in this area.
3. Ask yourself what fantasies play over and over in your mind that you wish your saved wife would perform that "Lip-luscious" did for you before. Have you completely given those thoughts to God and now watch and pray against the very appearance of them?
4. What deep hurts wake up when your husband or wife touches you in that spot that someone robbed or took from you? Are you reacting to your spouse in a positive way?
5. How much longer will you not speak of this to your husband or wife? Even the "woman with the issue of blood" ran to God to be healed.
6. What are you afraid of in your past or maybe what you expect for the future?
7. How long will you give the enemy room in your bedroom to steal, kill, and destroy your sanctuary? You are only victims of your thoughts when you give place to it and not bring it into the obedience of what God's Word has to say about these thoughts.

Chapter Two

Sex Has Many Advantages

Sex has many advantages, but let's look at some of the most important ones:
- Sex can relax you.
- Sex can bring you and your spouse closer both naturally and spiritually.
- Sex can bring forth children.
- Most of all, sex can help you deal with flesh and its temptations.

Sex is so powerful and by now you should have that concept down. But not only is it powerful, it has endless advantages for you and your spouse. A few that I feel have the most meaning and will bless you the most are described here, but I am sure you can write up a whole list of other advantages, too. To begin, it is important that you have God's Spirit, which teaches us all things, to instruct you on how to appreciate and use what I call "home court advantage." When I played sports, every time I came home for a Friday night game, it was on. The home crowd was there, we had a really a good team, the court was familiar, and no one could tell us we were going to lose. All the practice, sweat, and tears paid off and for many seasons, we went on to be undefeated. Take that same picture, come into the bedrooms of millions of Christian marriages today, and ask yourself, "Have I taken advantage of my sex life and am I using my own home court to my advantage? Or am I one of those Christians who have never taken advantage of our home court?"

Today, there are so many Christian couples walking around who find it hard to smile, laugh, and just simply enjoy the company of one another. Husbands are preoccupied with whatever they can find just to avoid the so-called nagging wife or the "not tonight" refusal again, or they no longer have an interest in having sex with their wives. Wives are overwhelmed, tired with chores and children, not to mention all the volunteer work at the school and the church. The constant pull to be the Proverbs 31 woman is just too much. She thinks, "Sex?! Please."

If you've had a hard day at work, exhaustion comes before the thought of a good night of sweat and scents of sex; at least from one of you. Then all of a sudden the unnecessary confusion steps in and the instant argument begins. But how many times have we as Christians been asked to do something we absolutely did not want to do, but we did it anyway because the pastor asked, someone was watching, and we felt it was our responsibility? Then, because of the dynamics of the situation, we dared not complain and did it all with a smile. Man, what if we could take that same instant "want to" and bring it into our bedrooms? Do you not understand that God judges your heart and not just your actions, and when you do something out of a heart of flesh, it is a sour smell to the nostrils of God? But even when you don't want to do something, like have sex with your spouse, you humble yourself and realize that if anybody is going to get the best of me even when I'm at my worst, it has to be my spouse (sacrifice).

We will wake up in the middle of the night for a random call of help, push ourselves to the limit of exhaustion to carry out a task pastor may ask done, and then come home and give our loved ones straight hell for them simply asking for something that belongs to them first. In my years of having a relationship with God, I have learned that I cannot give of myself beyond my ability to anyone else and not be a blessing to my own house. If I give and give to everyone outside of Judea (my home), my ministry, then everything about me is an abomination to the Lord. His Word declares that any man that cannot take care of his own home is worse than an infidel, and that is not just for men but women, too. Yes, you can volunteer, babysit, cook, work, and do whatever you feel you want to do, but your first ministry is to be a blessing to your own home.

Study the Proverbs 31 woman. She and her husband had a mutual relationship and he respected her enough to call her his favor. He was praised to be married to her. As busy as this woman was, even to the point of staying up all night, he still called her his and was able to say she brought him pleasure. So let me tell you, if cooking for the church is going to take you away from your ministry at home, you may want to let your pastor know.

Quit trying to please everybody outside your house and put your cooking clothes on and minister to your loved one. One thing about serving one another sexually: when you are able to be pleasing in the eyes of the one you love, you are truly pleasing the Lord more than when you give yourself to something you truly don't want to do.

The Bible declares that God uses the foolish things of this world to confound the wise, and until we realize that we operate on a different plain, sex will always be something that you get frustrated with instead of understand or enjoy. As complex as sex is, it's still not to be so complex that you can't understand it. Did it ever occur to you that if you both engage in sex, it will help with pressure and the tightness you feel running through you? Sex, for some of you, will even alleviate the very thought of cheating on your wife or husband. Just think about it. The enemy sends those arrows when you are absent from being sexually active with your loved one for a longer than usual time.

Sex has the power to help a person relieve all kinds of things going on in the body that you may not even be able to explain, from lowering blood pressure to alleviating aches and pains. Has it ever occurred to you that the best way for you to unwind is to allow sex to relax you both? How about instead of taking a pain pill, you put the children in the bed, lay with your spouse, cuddle, take your mind off of whatever is bothering you, rub each other down, massage temples, massage backs, turn down the lights, light a candle, don't talk, and just embrace? If you have to say what's hurting, say it, but give your spouse an opportunity to help you, heal.

The body can heal itself at times and sex is one of the ways it can help you sleep, while it heals. With great sex, calories are burned, energy is exerted, and you put your mind on something other than pain. Having regular sex can also help to relieve the stressors that you have to deal with on a day-to-day basis. Yes, we have the Spirit of God who gives us joy, peace, and helps us to relax, but God has also given us the gift of sex to help promote the intimacy in our marriage and relax us.

Sounds crazy, but the problem here is our way of thinking versus the Lord's way. You put everything before your spouse instead of learning how to really enjoy your spouse. You learn how to sew, knit, golf, play Madden, succeed at your job, raise children, pray, repair houses, repair cars, perform in-depth mathematical calculations, and never take the time to perfect your sex life. When was the last time you took a class or read a book on sex?

Why not? Who do you get your ideas from in this area? Or better yet, is this just your way of doing things? I wonder why a doctor can go to school for years and feel they have achieved the American dream. Then, when she comes home, the very thing that holds her to her husband is never once considered as nearly as important as her career or life outside the house. Both parties wonder where they went wrong or how the other person could cheat or no longer satisfy the other. Well, how much time have you spent in sowing into this area? When you make love with your wife or husband, is it just like the drive-thru, quick and demanding? Have you ever tried to relax and just enjoy yourself or is everything always about the other person operating and being in charge? Who is doing all the work? What are you doing? Do you just lay there or are you involved?

Do you not enjoy sex because you have no clue as to what you are doing? When you have sex, do you have fun? Is it enough during the week for you and your spouse? How do you know if his cup is running over or not? Have you asked him, "Honey, have you had enough; do you need more?" Is foreplay even in the picture when you both are together? Do you sit down to a fully fledged feast each night or eat just enough and turn around in a matter of minutes and desire more? Whatever way you engage in this activity, no matter how you try to be discrete and hide your true feelings toward one another, it will be shown when you are with your spouse in public. People can tell genuine couples in love and when the bedroom is being taking care of, for the very thing that brings you joy and rest in life also puts on a smile on your face at just the mention of it. There is a big difference when you are passionate about someone versus going through the motions. Passion is an intense emotion, just like love, hatred, joy, or even anger. Jesus Christ was passionate for this world in that He gave Himself for it. Are you passionately in love with your spouse or just going through the motions?

When I talk about the sex between my husband and me, as secretive as it is, I must admit that we have an incredible sex life. As far as all the details, they are not important to you because what works for me will not necessarily work for you.

We are all human beings, but because of gravity and the makeup of each human being, sex is an experience each couple has to be willing to explore to learn how to enjoy one another. Let me just make this point clear: you cannot expect to pass any test by just staying up one night and then saying, "Okay, that's it." No, you are going to have to invest and set aside some time to learn how to be successful in something that means so much to the one you love. You seem to be able to do everything with a whole heart, but when it comes to sex, it's just whatever. You don't say it, but it shows because you don't take the time to do the homework on what you can and cannot do in your bedroom. Only through communication with one another and prayer in the Lord can you find out what is acceptable and what is not.

Just like a football team, each team has a different set of plays for the person who will be responsible for carrying them out. But when we incorporate our abilities and find out just how to operate as a team during this play, we are able to rejoice knowing that we both score a touchdown together. Sex is not a selfish act when you both are actively engaged in it and take the time to learn what pleases you both. *If sex is not fun to you or you have no interest in it at all, that is a direct reflection of its importance in your life or the life of your spouse. It is also a great indicator to the importance of your relationship with one another.*

When I first started going out on Saturdays witnessing to people needing Jesus in their lives, I didn't like it because of so many dynamics taking place right in front of my face. Due to unfavorable conditions, I was surprised at how some people could live this way, but they did. Those Saturdays were our family times and I had to go do this? I did a lot of complaining at first, but I wanted to do exactly what God was asking me to do. I can hear my own Spirit crying out "go." Each time I went out, it made me that much more sensitive to the fact that God really needed me to help these people. When we would finally get started, I never wanted to leave. So many times I remember thinking if I could just enjoy the moment I would be able to deny myself, the way I looked and felt about witnessing, and really see people receive the Lord in such a wretched place. I could enjoy and learn what I was supposed to learn while I was taking apart of this great assignment for God.

In like manner, making love to your spouse is also another form of ministry. As a woman who loves God with all her heart, I love my husband so much. I want to be a part of what is important to him. Granted, I get tired, but those are the times I boldly confess, "God, it is You who is working in me even now to do the will of the Father, to do of His good pleasure, and I am not going to murmur or complain but I am going to submit myself and enjoy this very moment. Not my will, Lord, but Thy will be done and if this is what you are giving to my spouse at this moment to do, at this very hour, increase me, teach me, and show me how to be all you have called me to be and more in this bedroom. What does it profit me to bring glory and get someone saved when I leave the house and when my husband asks me to make love to him at home, I am not able to walk in that same power? The devil is a liar and the very father of them. Now, it's time to pray for the power of God to help me enjoy my husband and that his cup would overflow. If anybody is going to have a testimony of how good God is, it is going to be my husband.

Men are born to produce. Whether it's working or having sex, it is a natural part of being a man. So when you get married, if you don't know that sex is to be an expected part of the picture, stay tuned; you'll soon find out. If you wanted to cast down imaginations and shy from the very presence of sex, you may have a single mindset because that is not the way of those who are happily married. As married couples, we are to expect sex—great sex—because it is the way we as humans continue to survive today. A sad picture to see is the couple who shares no desire for one another just living together and having no appetite for each other anymore.

Even for me, sex has not always been this way, but I have never lost sight of this beautiful specimen God has entrusted unto me. Daily I tell him how wonderful he makes me feel and how much I absolutely need every part of his body. Even if we don't end up making love, just to tell him how wonderful he makes me feel lets him know I still desire him. I make it a habit to ensure that he knows he is fully satisfying me and that I find him completely breathtaking after a night of lovemaking. I know this helps him to know he is doing the right thing and I do enjoy him. Your husband may not say it, but when a woman can express to her husband that he is bringing pleasure and there is absolutely no one else to replace him, these things have an astounding effect on the way a man sees himself and how he sees you. Men need admiration and, most of all, they need to hear you say how much you really enjoy what they are providing for you, in and out of the bedroom. That in itself is a turn-on for any man.

Some men have had to grow up not hearing a woman say, "Well done, son; you did an awesome job!" Go ahead and ring that bell for your husband. You can thank me later. Remember you have what you say, so watch what you speak on your husband's life, too. Never speak negativity prior to or during sex, but pray. Although he's not Mr. Romeo, he does something's right, he chose you, so give him credit for that. Pray about the good things you see your husband doing and even while you are getting ready for a night of pleasure, start confessing how wonderful your husband is and how you expect to have a night of magic. Speak directly to his body parts and how you expect them to bring you pleasure all the days of your life. Get excited about sex and watch the very atmosphere change in your bedroom.

Relaxation is a time for you and your husband to learn to celebrate one another while you have each other here on earth. Stop living as if you have your whole life with this person, as no one is promised tomorrow. Our days are as grass: here today and gone tomorrow. Enjoy one another while you can. Stop taking one another for granted and learn to understand the one you dwell with. Learning to relax when you engage in sex is not just for the one you love, but for you, too. Make time and find out what your spouse needs and make it your business to be pleasing in his/her eyes, fill his/her cup up. Money is great, games are recreational, but when a husband and wife come together to have sex, the ability for them to release can leave both of them speechless. There is no greater sleep than after a night of passionate lovemaking.

My husband and I have young children, so it is a mandate every night that all children are asleep or going to bed before 8:00 p.m. so that he and I can spend that quality time. This time is not for bills or individual things unless we decide we are not going to spend that time doing something together. But whatever we do, we leave this time for the two of us to be able to minister to one another in whatever capacity is needed. Do we always get to climb the ceiling or be as romantic as we would like? Of course not, but we do make time and realize that just like anything else in our relationship, it all must be given attention.

A song was once written that talked about sex and its healing power. Does "Sexual Healing" by Marvin Gaye ring any bells? Okay, it's not a Christian song, but even Balaam's donkey was used by the Lord to speak the truth. If you have never heard this song and one day get a chance to, you will agree that sexual lovemaking is a form of healing for the both of you, especially the man. When you take the time to really cherish, learn, operate, and enjoy what you have, this great act of sex with your spouse can really become an act you both look forward to. While you both are able to relax and realize sex was made for both of you to enjoy, you'll go out of your way to make it enjoyable. Sex was never made to be a hindrance in your marriage, but a help.

If you were to take a picture of some of the couples in church today, the pictures would probably look like a commercial for some kind of sour lemonade. What is really going on behind closed doors and who is having sex and enjoying it anymore? What excuses will you have to keep making to avoid this act sent from heaven? Here is a good excuse from couples who are not passionately in love with one another anymore, and when they see a couple smiling and embracing after church say, "It doesn't take all of that and that's simply flesh on parade. When we were young, we were like that!" But let me ask you something, what part of your body is old? I know you have heard this one before when you see a couple all lovey-dovey: "They are just young; wait until they get older!" What kind of person would say something like that? Someone who is not involved in the act themselves or someone who has forgotten how wonderful sex was for them at one time.

If you are having sex and you are not relaxed, my question is: what are you doing or not doing when are you doing what you're doing, and when do you plan to take the time to learn how to relax and enjoy yourself? Really, how close are you and your spouse now that you have put sex on the backburner—oh, excuse me—in the freezer? Why does it seem as if there is a belief we have allowed as a body that unless you are young and hot you can't honestly be enjoying yourself and eventually the lust will wear off and real love with come forth? That's straight from the devil and anyone who speaks of this is being used by the devil. As a matter of fact, just look at their marriage and see if there is anything you could possibly learn from them, and then run!

Sex Can Bring You and Your Spouse Closer both Naturally and Spiritually.

Let's look at a few reasons why, when you engage in sex, you become one flesh, a powerful union in the eyes of God, and an absolute threat to the enemy. If Satan can get us to stop having sex as married people, there will be no more God-fearing children, no more deposits into one another.

Sex has a way of bringing the emotions, feelings, concerns, touches, and most of all, intimacy together in ways one could only imagine. Yes, as couples you touch, talk, and kiss, but there is union that's taking place in which the both of you become emptied. You share a common ground, a secret place, a trust, and a reservoir that only you and your spouse can access. Although the world takes and takes of you, this one thing is shared with only the one you love. You have complete control as to how you will give and receive.

This is an area that God has said, "Son and daughter, enjoy yourselves and be fruitful and multiply. There were no stipulations to this act; just become one in the eyes of God and enjoy your wife or husband." My husband sees my flaws and knows it's not about the scars from the c-section, the cuts on my leg, fat hanging here and there, the layers around this or that, but he sees that I'm willing to continue to come to him and allow him to enjoy himself and be himself. This is the place where who I am becomes completely transparent.

Transparency during sex is a must in order to have great sex. If you have a problem with the light, say it. If you think you are fat, tell him. If you are having problems keeping up, speak it. If you get tired quickly, say it. If you hurt, say it. If you don't like a position, say it. If you don't think it's a good time, but you can make another time, say it. But do whatever you do in order to grow and to learn of one another. Open up your mouth and learn who is sleeping next to you. Couples spend years together only to come to the end of the road and ask, "Who are you?"

When we as the body of Christ can begin to be transparent with ourselves and our spouses, we can truly begin to heal in this area of sex. For a long time in our early years of marriage, after having children,

I didn't like the way my stomach looked. I use to always buy lingerie that hid my stomach or tried to get in some kind of position to try and hide it. One day, my husband told me to turn on the light. He told me how beautiful I was and that it was time to stop trying to hide the scars because they were never going anywhere and neither was he.

I remember crying in his arms and telling him how I had more insecurities that kept me from really being more expressive in bed and how if I could change a few things or take a few things back or exercise more or just do whatever to be a better me, our sex life would be better. He took my hand, took the anointing oil in our bedroom and put it all over me, and said, "There is nothing wrong with your body as far as I am concerned. If you are too big, I will help you lose weight. If you don't like something, I will help you pray about it. But whatever you do, don't complain about what my Father has made and who you are in my life. Each time you complain it makes me feel as if I am less than a man and that I am married to just anything. The devil is a liar."

Rubbing the oil all over me and praying, he reaffirmed to me that if I was willing to accept what has happened in life, how I was made, to never compare myself to anyone, and to begin to thank God for giving me insight and wisdom, not only would I enjoy who I was, but he would be able to enjoy me all the more. Naturally, I was hurt and embarrassed, but I told my husband how I really felt in the room and what I thought he saw when he looked at me. I never really asked him up until then what his picture of me was.

In his eyes, I was anointed and a woman of God who had given my body over to have children and had had some mishaps, but that all the flaws and pictures of me could never replace the joy he had experienced in having children and being married to me. In the natural, sex is the closeness God allows the both of you to experience naked and unashamed.

In our natural states, you have to learn how to appreciate what you have and look at your past scars, hurts, and pains as victories you have overcome. Just because you got a little big doesn't mean you can't do something about it; don't just make excuses and complain. Just because somebody next door or in the church is more shapely than you doesn't mean you can't take control of your body and ask God to help you see what your loved ones sees when he or she looks at you. Stop allowing the devil to feed your insecurities.

In the natural, you are what you say you are, and if all you do is put yourself down, what loved one can find that attractive? Newsflash: a man is attracted to a woman who is still worth the chase. Some years after getting past that hump, I began to hold my head up high, scars and all, and say, "Honey, this is me and this is the best you will get." I pull out the g-strings, t-shirts, edible things, and anything I can find to blow this man's mind. Whatever I have to do to make sure this man is completely satisfied naturally, I will do.

So, I may have this or that going on, but as long as I can work everything else and put a smile on his face, then I am going to do it, so help me God. Never allow the devil to set up any barriers concerning your bedroom. The Lord tells us that marriage is honorable and that you are to keep your bedrooms undefiled. Tell the devil as long as my spouse is pleased, you can take those suggestions and ideas about who you think I ought to be and go straight to hell with them.

Just to silence the devil and his plans even now, know that on top of looking like you desire to look and dressing up when you come in the bedroom, Pastor Lester Sumrall advises couples that "no kind of sexual pleasure is 'off limits' to husband and wife, as long as it honors the God in each of you." Some people think that only one particular technique of lovemaking is "holy" and all others are sinful, but you won't find teaching like that anywhere in the Bible, only to enjoy one another and produce. While everyone is so busy trying to figure out if it's all wrong, just make the time to get together and explore one another.

Having sex and achieving an orgasm will increase your levels of the hormone oxytocin. What many call the "love hormone," oxytocin helps you both to bond and build trust with one another. Having higher levels of oxytocin will allow you to feel the urge to nurture and to bond more compassionately.

Need ideas? Read and educate yourself on the book of Song of Solomon for starters. Read it in several translations, look up the words, and you will be amazed as married people what you should be engaging in. We tell our fellow brothers in church that whatever is in the Word we live by and leave the whole book, Song of Solomon, out. Go to the library and check out books that help explain more in detail about the makeup of your spouse's body. Make it your business to find out what feels good and was doesn't and, most of all, just ask. Go ahead; light some candles, pull your lingerie out, and open Song of Solomon. Start reading to one another, even if your spouse is not in the Lord yet, and start with the Message Bible translation. You'll be surprised at how much your spouse already understands about the topics discussed. Remember just by reading you are planting seeds into the one you love and in time, you will reap harvest because you took the time to sow the word into their life.

You have to start somewhere, and where your spouse is makes all the difference. Push past everything and get all that belongs to you. Try it out and see; the more sex you have the more you desire, but the less sex you have the less you desire.

Spiritually, having sex births pleasure between you in ways you could never imagine. Not only do you share the bed, you become one flesh. You think like each other at times; it makes the intimacy between you like concrete, in which almost nothing can get between. It allows you to become one about some of your deepest concerns with yourself and feel safe as you share your true feelings with the one you love. Not only do you share your life with a God who knows all, when you are intimate with God daily, He steps in and intervenes in your bedroom. I may be a writer, but honestly this can't even be explained. Trying to explain sex spiritually is like trying to explain the glory of God.

In my best words, and what I believe God is telling you even now, is if you want a night filled with pleasure, ask God to endow you with the power to please your wife or husband like nothing he or she has ever experienced. I promise if you pray and believe, God will give you nights that have had to come from heaven itself. If you don't know how to be creative, ask God to give you creative nights, unimaginable energy, and a sweet smell of lovemaking that will fill your room from dusk until dawn. Yes, sex is powerful, but God is all-powerful. Spiritually, as you submit to one another and really take the marriage as serious as any other part of ministry, you begin to expect a great sex life. I truly believe as saints that everything we touch can become paramount when we lay hands on it.

Some of my most memorable nights are when my husband and I have had the time to really talk to one another prior to sex, made sure we agreed not to get mad, and went to bed always cuddling. In other words, we would not allow one another to get offended or upset without praying and asking God to be in the midst. If things became too overwhelming, or if it was going the wrong way, we needed to stop, love on one another, and say, "That's enough," and finish it again on another night after praying.

This is not the time to give place to the devil, when you are allowing each other's ground to be tilled. The Bible tells us to shake up our fallow ground and therefore in the Spirit we can use this time to really hear what's on the hearts of our spouses and begin to pray and intercede to help fight on behalf of the ones we love. What person who really loves his spouse would just let the other person bleed to death and offer no bandage?

Knowing how to have sex and build intimacy is twofold, but intimacy is most important. Intimacy is several things: a close relationship, a quiet atmosphere, and detailed knowledge you both share concerning one another. But most of all, it is the freedom to explore one another with no strings attached and no rules involved, nothing but pure motives to uncover all the hidden potential you both have to offer one another both naturally and spiritually. Building intimacy in your marriage is as critical as laying foundation for any home. When you don't have this foundation, intimacy with one another, cracks, rips, and tears in your relationship can wear you down. But thanks to God, although we live in mortal bodies, we are temples of the living God. We understand balance and, most of all, we understand that it is God's Spirit which is able to draw us closer in ways the natural man will never be able to even understand.

So yes, sex is an act that takes place in the natural, but God has given us free reign in this area. With His Spirit as our guide, we are instructed to dwell with one another according to knowledge, which, simply put, means to know what each other's needs are, both naturally and spiritually, and meet them.

<u>Sex Brings Forth Children</u>

This is a sensitive aspect of sex that many, including myself, have even dared to discuss: having children. Many Christians may be sexually active and still not able to conceive. To me, nothing hurts more than to see many people having children and know that you cannot have any. I always believe that, even in this area, you have to take this issue to God and, like Hanna, demand a yes or no. Even with my own children, they can understand no when I explain to them my reasons why. We have a Father, Jesus Christ, who will give peace when couples are barren. Whatever His reasons, I truly believe God will speak to your heart when it comes to not having children. It is His will that we all be fruitful and multiply, and when this is a trial for many, like any other situation that is contrary to the Word of God, we have to be on our faces in prayer until, like Jacob, the Lord blesses us with an answer.

In my first marriage, I was barren for the duration of our two-year union. Many years before, I had an operation that took a toll on me and the doctors continued to say it would be a miracle if I had children, but somehow I still believed. It hurt me every day that I could not give this man children. In my mind, I thought having children might keep the rascal at home, but thank God even in this situation, no children were born out of this marriage. I soon gave up on having children with this man, accepted my fate as being a barren woman, and shortly after, got divorced. On the flipside of this confession, I really wanted children, but that desire did not come full circle until I met my second husband, who I love with every inch of my being.

When I met Walter, there was no way I was not having this man's babies. Everything about him spelled "father." His life had to be birthed into our children and there was no way I would live on this earth with him and not have his children. In my previous marriage, I didn't care anymore that we didn't have children, but with this man, my determination changed.

Even my desire became relentless and my confession began to speak exactly what God said I could have, children in due season. In prayer, after giving my life to the Lord and marrying Walter, I began to ask God for his children to come forth and whatever was holding them back to be removed. I will never forget this day in Chattanooga, Tennessee, on a cold winter afternoon, I heard the Lord say, "Your first child shall be called Walter Jr., a warrior sent by God."

My husband and I were in a hotel to celebrate our upcoming birthdays and one year anniversary that night, and although I had been sexually active for a while in my young life, this would be the first time ever that I would have to say that God was in complete control. Everything was just perfect. The hotel room was beautiful, the night clothing was all Victoria's Secret, the scent of both of us was my favorite smell and his favorite smell, and no detail was left undone, down to the food. This night was more unimaginable than our wedding night. Something special was unfolding right before my eyes and I was aware of it all.

God took my mind, my confession, and my whole outlook of sex to another level. In an instant, what I thought sex and lovemaking was supposed to be I was looking at in a whole different way. This night was not going to be another night of sex as usual. This was not going to be a night to show and see who could do what and that was it. It would be a night that I would live to see the power of God operating in our bedroom. My husband was willing to be gentle, take the time to understand my body, and what was pleasing to me.

He prayed over the whole room prior to lovemaking and then he prayed over my body and asked God to open up my matrix in a way that only God could do Himself. He let me know that he was no other man and that I should never compare him or his lovemaking ability, but to embrace exactly who he was. He asked me to relax and allow God to be God in our marriage. He put my mind at ease, that whether we had children or not, his love for me was here to stay. He reassured me that children would not add or take away from the love that he had for me. If we never had children, I would still be Mrs. Christy Kirkland. For the first time in my life, I felt free enough to allow a man to go to a place I thought was never possible, even in marriage.

It's sad for couples to be married and not able to enjoy one another because of past hurts, pains, expectations, hidden motives, or even comparisons taking place right during the act of sex. So many small factors that are critical to powerful sex go unnoticed. Then we get in church and pay attention to every detail and walk blindsided in our bedrooms. During this time, I had absolutely no regrets and no thoughts of what-ifs, no thoughts of what could hurt, or even if he knew what he was doing, but in this very hour, I put my total trust in the Lord that He had equipped this man just for me and I was going to enjoy him all the days of my life, children or not. It didn't even matter anymore because the very thing that I thought was so important to me I was allowing to kill the vision of what was important to him.

I allowed this man of God to be used by God and I was about to dive completely in his trust and I didn't care how deep the water was or if he could not catch me. After years of pain, doubt, and never knowing whether I would be able to have children, nine months later, Walter Lee Kirkland, Jr. was born. Following that, I would have another son, William Princeton Kirkland, and then my little angel, Elisabeth Rose Kirkland. God is still in the miracle working business even in your bedroom and children are still a part of His plan for your marriage. Only believe and trust that in due season, you shall reap if you faint not. Don't allow situations to dictate a move of God that He has orchestrated just for you.

To all the couples who cannot produce, present that case to the Lord. Ask Him if it is His desire that you have children. And if it is, and it is, then declare and rebuke Satan today. You are married, you are right in the sight of God, He has ordained this act, your male and female organs are supposed to be responding, and you are supposed to produce. So if you have to wait, wait in faith and nothing wavering. But at least make sure you are not giving any glory to the devil by complaining, doubting, or believing that your womb is cursed.

Even now, pray this prayer over yourself if you so desire children and believe God:

Lord, I declare that above all, I am blessed and highly favored. I am Your righteousness, and I am full of Your Spirit. I declare that the fruit of my womb is blessed, and I am blessed to have a quiver full of children as the Lord sees fit. I am a child of God and I shall have what I say according to the Word of God. I believe that this body belongs to God and He can have His way with it any way He desires and if it is His good pleasure that I be fruitful and multiply, then I receive all God has for me. Now Satan, my husband and I bind you in the name of Jesus and decree we are loosed from not being able to produce.

Take your hands off my mind and take your hands off this land. We shall be able to bring forth children, as many as the Lord would allow us to have. As for me, we shall live to see abundance and be blessed with children in the name of Jesus Christ. I am naming my children right now. (Begin to call the names into the atmosphere and let God know you are walking by faith and will not give place to any devil in your bedroom.) Amen.

To shame the devil and really be a bold witness for the Lord, forget about having children right now and just enjoy one another while God makes a fool out of the enemy. When you are not able to have children and you focus on the thought of having children so much, you don't focus on enjoying the process of conceiving them. I went through this with my husband and when I was finally able to take my mind off having children, walk by faith, and finally stand my ground on what already belongs to me, we were blessed with three children. I never stop believing and I began to call each of my children out by name. All our battles with the enemy are spiritual, and we cannot allow ourselves to take sex out of the equation, thinking it's an area that we can conquer without praying about it.

To many who have legitimate medical or physiological problems in having children, God is still a healer. Over and over, we see couples who were barren in the bible as well as today, for whatever reason, yet believe God. Eventually, in Gods time the couple was able to give birth, for example, Abraham and Sarah, Elisabeth and Zechariah and even me. Christians are instructed to walk and live by faith in order to please God. So what people may be having children left and right around you, God knows exactly what He is doing in a person life. If waiting will increase your faith or cause you to believe again, or even draw closer to the Father, you may have to wait.

Maybe there is unresolved sin lingering, like Micah who was King Saul's daughter, she had a problem with David expressing himself before the Lord, the Lord caused her womb to cease from ever having kids. Sarah, Abraham's wife, wanted to go about bringing her promise to past and did what she thought was the right way of having children and today, we are reaping that bad decision. If you haven't been able to conceive, don't just throw in the towel, go on a fast, pray, and seek God like never before for an answer regarding this decision.

Get aggressive and cry out to the Lord for an answer. Jacob wrestled with the Lord all night until he was blessed and received an answer of the Lord. How desperate are you and what have you done to show you both are standing and believing on Word of God. Do you have names already? Faith says, I already have, what I am believing God for.

What has the Lord spoken to you regarding this area? Are you both in agreement to having children and how do you know? What areas in your spouse life may be hindering a move of God that you both have not discussed? God has promised if we seek His face, He will answer us. Has He told you no, or have your situation, doctors report, and life simple given you the final answer? Whose report are you going to believe? When are you going to walk by faith inspite of what of what life says? Lay hands on your bible and declare, "Lord, I will not let you go, until you bless me, and if you see fit otherwise, you will tell me this also."

Confess this daily, with your spouse and especially before and after having sex, if you are desiring children: 1 John 5:14-15 declares, "And this is the boldness which we have toward him, that, if we ask anything according to his will, he heareth us: and if we know that he heareth us whatsoever we ask, we know that we have the petitions which we have asked of him."

Sex Helps You Deal with Everyday Flesh and Temptations

How much sex is enough sex? I'm glad you asked! No man can put a number on this area except you and your spouse. If you know about grass, there are all kinds. Depending on the type of grass you have, will determine the type of care you will give, in order for it to grow its best. Why? Grass grows different in different environments and like couples, they to grow differently compared to others. If you have too much sun, growers instruct you to use certain seeds and fertilizers. But if you have no sun, they have something for that, too, just like in our relationship, we have to know what we need to continue to grow and be satisfied completely. When you are lacking or not getting enough sex in the bedroom, you have to let the other person know in love so they can meet your needs. Never turn to another human being outside your bedroom to give you advice as to how much sex is enough. They do not know your makeup or what you may be experiencing when you both are together.

To put a number on sex in the bedroom just doesn't make sense to me because everyone is different. If you desire to have sex for only two times a week and your spouse is happy with that, amen. Or maybe, you chose to have sex daily, its up to you and your spouse to determine what will be healthy for your relationship to be sustained. I believe deciding how much sex is enough comes from, the Holy Ghost and your spouse. But whatever it is, you best believe you better understand what kind of grass you've got growing before you decide the grass is greener on the other side.

Understand this: when you are satisfied in the bedroom at home, the enemy can send all kinds of temptations your way and it doesn't wake up or tempt anything in you. But the minute you have gone too long without this wonderful act of sex, your fertilizer, your sun, your water, and everything else you want to call this essential need in your life, all kinds of ideas will come to mind. This is why when you and your spouse are not having sex, it must be an agreement between the both of you and as soon as you come back make sure you carry out this act.

Satan doesn't play fair; he sends everything your way just to see if you are in a place to be taken advantage of when you are vulnerable. See, when you are not getting your daily essential needs and the Lord is not keeping you, you will get your daily essentials from anyone. We hear from many couples who cannot believe their husband cheated on them with someone who was just the opposite of them. But when you haven't drunk from your own cistern, water needed in a drought is good no matter how it comes out, as long as it comes out. But we are instructed to drink water from our own cistern. Temptations only come when you are lacking in what you believe you need and an opportunity presents itself which is contrary to the will of God.

The devil knows how powerful the act of sex can be because he used this tactic before and has seen the effects on humankind. Do you not think he will use it on you? In the garden, Adam was busy naming all kinds of creatures and probably spent most of his day walking, trying to find them. Then he had to spend time talking with God about what to call the animals. Can you imagine that job? You see something come out of the water and you say fish, then you see another animal and what are you going to call that? Then another something is biting you on the feet and the bite feels like fire, so it must be a fire ant. All day he was talking and thinking, and just maybe he ran out of words to say to his wife when he came home.

But his wife needed communication and she found it from Satan. No matter how much you give outside your home, when you come home, you have to still meet the needs of those you live with. It is imperative that you save some of your time and energy to be of use when you come home because the minute you are too tired or so-called drained, it is too easy for the enemy to open up a flowing source. It will only take a minute for the one that will look appealing to the eye and be all you miss at home. Eve spent her time getting affection from another man to the point that she trusted in what he had to offer.

That was a relationship that had been built over some time of talking and meeting with this force. Somebody who was listening and making time to give her what her husband was falling short in. Temptations in sex work both ways whether you are at home or on the job. Don't think that just because you are at home that you are free from temptations, and vice versa for the person working outside the home.

Temptations come tailor-made from the enemy himself and, after studying you, will appear to be exactly what you supposedly need and what is sent from God.

Paul instructs us as married people to be in agreement if you are not engaging in sex together, lest the devil come and tempt us (1 Corinthians 7:5). God has given us so much freedom in this area that to be spiritual in the bedroom is almost inappropriate, but you must be. Yes, it sounds like a contradiction, but believe me; it's not. In the same sense that you are spiritual, you have to use the wisdom of God to operate with your body *and* soul. Sex is a gift that God has given to the human race to enjoy and speak to him about. In the same sense where there is freedom, he still instructs you to pray about your sexual acts in the bedroom. As a Christian, the only person you need to discuss your acts in the bedroom with is your husband or wife and God. If you are sharing your bedroom with anyone else, make sure it's something that only God has instructed you to do.

So many people feel spiritually connected when they meet somebody who's going through what they are going through. A sister in the church finds companionship with another man in the church or on the job who is going through what she is experiencing: a setup from the enemy. How can you get help from someone else bleeding? We have a Father who in all points was tempted but was without sin and even in that understands whatever it is that we are going through.

You should never share your diary with someone who supposedly understands, but share your diary with a God who can change your situation as well as cause deliverance to come to your house.

If you have someone to talk to about your sexual concerns, he or she should possess the following: a personal relationship with Jesus Christ and freedom of self opinions; training in this area; his or her own fruit-bearing marriage; openness that welcomes the discussion of sex with you, not shying away from the topic; freedom to talk about what the Lord has done for his or her sex life; a calling from God to minister to you in this area; a prayer life; and willingness to receive the Lord to carry you and your husband or wife over to a place where God can give you help. Calling your mother, sister, or best friend, who have none of these qualities, is a train wreck waiting to happen.

Stop asking what people think who have no idea what you do or want to do. Stop expecting people to tell you exactly what is going to work in your bedroom. God has given that sacred place to you and your spouse and He expects you to have full dominion over it. Whatever shortcoming you or your spouse have regarding sex, pray about those issues together and by yourself until the Lord sends peace in that area. If you are going to be spiritual about anything regarding this area, be spiritual enough to know that God sets the standard through the married couple about what goes on in your bedroom.

If you want to be super creative in your bedroom and spice it up tonight, speak with your husband openly about it and then pray to the Lord to give you the desire to perform it. If you want this or want to do that, pray and ask God so that your motives are to please your husband or wife and not wake up something that would cause confusion in your home over past experiences that God has delivered you from. Make sure you are not trying to defile something God has called holy. "How can two walk, except they be agreed?" (Amos 3:3). Maybe you need to remove any crazy desires from your mind altogether if they keep trying to sabotage your bedroom. God can remove those thoughts and give you new ones.

Whatever it is that keeps you from running to your bedroom and not expecting, ask God to help you fulfill the needs of the one you love. Maybe it's you that is the problem and you can't understand why. Ask God to help reveal yourself and allow you to see just how you are in the bedroom. He will show you why sex to you or your spouse is not fun, relaxing, enough, great, or why you could just do without it. But if it's important to your husband or wife and really matters a lot, you must learn all you can to be found pleasing in the eyes of the one you love. God is the master of all marriage matters, including sex.

"So ought men to love their wives as their own bodies. He that loveth his wife loveth himself. For no man ever yet hated his own flesh; but noursiheth and cherisheth it, even as the Lord the church. (Eph 5:28-29)." A happy man is a happy woman. Most happy men have great sex at home and most happy women enjoy the sex with their husband. Both parties understand the importance the role plays in their lives and when sexual activity takes place, it's not just something either one of you do to fulfill your duties, but it is recreational and inviting for the both of you. It is also a chance to fulfill the needs of each other. "How can two walk except they are agreed?" (Amos 3:3). Taking the time to out to learn how to please your wife or husband in this area is a way of winning over another person completely. It shows you are taking the time to learn what the other person wants and ways to be successful in that area.

If you invest in yourself as an employee to get educated and become the subject matter expert in your field, in order to help the company advance as well as yourself, how much more should you invest to become knowledgable in your own relationship and advance your family? Let's look at how a person can deal with a dead end job and stick with it versus a marriage they feel is dead. We hear all the time, that one of the many reasons couples venture outside of marriage has all to do with their needs not being met. Let me ask you something, where else are your needs not being met but you still give it your all? There should never be a reason to have an extra martial affair. On any given day, you put up with disrespect, cursing, fussing, family separation, long hours, and all kinds of things at your job but its never enough to make you throw in the towel or seek employment elsewhere.

Well, why cheat on your spouse? Just because the corporation seems to be standing with people giving their time, advancement coming to you left and right, praise and admiration spoken, and your check seems secure, everything in this earth is going to pass away and that is a promise. Only what you do and give to God, (remember your spouse is created and made in the very image of God) will last. You may have a check today but one touch in your mortal body [like Job] and the very job you give your life to, will not even pay for you on your death bed. Ironic as it may seem, the very person you give your all to, each day regardless of the hardship you endure in marriage, will be there until death do you apart.

Invest in your marriage by reading educational sex books and or materials, but only after seeking God first. If you do this first, no matter what book you get, God will keep your mind and your heart stayed on Him. Do not be afraid to sow into your marriage because fear is not of God. God doesn't want you dumb or ignorant in life and most of all, desires that you get an understanding. As you begin to read yourself into a better marriage, God has a way of convicting His children, leading, and guiding you to those things that are pure and undefiled. No man, no matter where you are, fully knows what he is capable of, even if you feel super strong in the Lord, without the Lords leading, you can become vexed, and deceived if you allow yourself to dictate what you are going to read and sow into your marriage. What may feel good is not necessarily good for you.

Get educated but first start with your bible in this area, as you pray to God, to help you to guard your heart and your mind while reading. Satan is crafty and if you are weak when it comes to the area of sex, reading sex books can only complicate this area for you and your spouse. If reading books with nudity is a conviction for you, you need to find another way to educate yourself until or if God ever does, give you a release to do this. As a people of God, we have to be wise as serpents when we operate in this world and be certain not to operate by the world's way of doing things, even in our bedroom.

Porn or pornography, isn't educational, nor is it in anyway a means to glorify God. As Christians, you have to understand that the only nudity that God allowed in the beginning was that of Adam and Eve and during that time, sin had not come upon either of them (see Gen3:7). Adam and Eve walked daily before the Lord naked and unashamed but the minute they became guilty of sin and realized they were naked, they desired to cover themselves. So, today, we clothe ourselves knowing our sinful nature as human being will never be complete until we are like Jesus Christ in Heaven. Although, we are clothed with His righteousness, we are still spirits living in flesh bodies, and we possess a sinful nature. If we did not have the Spirit of God in us, God would not even look upon us as His own. We are instructed to put ye on Christ and clothe ourselves both spiritually as well as naturally. All the while, watching what our eyes are fixed upon.

I had to come this route to address this point, many wives deal with nudity issues, in their own home and this simple act of embarrassment can cause the husband great pain. Sweetheart, you go to the doctor and do all kinds of routines concerning your body, but when it comes to sex, you miss the whole picture. Doctors don't know you from Jump Street, but when you are asked to expose this or show that, you do it thinking they will be able to diagnose something or help you. But when you come to your bedroom, you feel as if you are being asked to perform open heart surgery. All your loved one wants is for you to trust them when they say you are beautiful and you do have all they need. Getting into a certain position is what they want and it has nothing to do with how you look or what they will think of you later. They are not lying when they tell you that your fat, meat, and other parts you find displeasing are beautiful to them.

But so many wives even in the body of Christ hide or are embarrassed about how they look and what their husbands are going to say, but just two days ago showed their total body parts to a man who God only knows what he thought about you. Stand in the mirror and look at yourself and what God has created. He said it was good; what are you confessing? Put on something sexy, fix your hair, and most of all, asks God to help you to renew your mind about what you see when you look at you. Confess you are beautiful and all your imperfection is being perfected in God. Let me tell you, even if you have a problem with it, just think that if your husband loves the way you get dressed up just for him, then keep on doing what you are doing because he finds pleasure in you doing this. You are not only making yourself look good, you are making him feel special by going out of your way just to lay with your spouse.

Yes it is a sin to look upon a fair woman and lust, but when it's your wife, it's okay to be tempted, to be enticed, and to be ravished. Tell your husband or your wife just how much you enjoy all of them and the way that they are able to please you in this area as well as others.

This is the part of your life where it is absolutely okay to build up the ego of a man *or* a woman. Men love admiration and respect shown to them and women love the appreciation given to them on a daily basis. Words are Spirit, and sometimes we forget that, even during sex, we can speak those things which may not be so, but believe God will bring them to pass in your life. So he's not Romeo; he is tonight. She is not some supermodel carved out of the magazine; by your own words, you have what you say—she is tonight and more. So a man believeth in his heart, so is he? This is your beloved and the one to whom God said, "Do what is pleasing to you both." Take pride in one another, their gifts and talents, realizing what you have but do not idolize your spouse. He or she is just a mere human made in God's image in which God has entrusted you with. Worship the Lord and his marvelous work and not the creature.

As much as I can think about it or even when I get in the bed, I begin to say, "Lord, cause my mind to be creative in this area of sex so I can do things which will help my husband enjoy sex with me. *Make our bedroom experiences lasting ones and most of all, Lord, don't let my husband leave this bedroom not one day unsatisfied, but most of all, hungry for more, in Jesus' name Help us to explore places and groves, we have never experienced as a couple. Father, let this man look forward to coming, to his garden. Amen*"

Sexual intimacy between you and your spouse is what you believe and make it to be in your bedroom. It is so sad to see people work hard on a daily basis for the praise of people who care absolutely nothing for them. Okay, you're paid at work for working hard, but when you work overtime at home, there is a reward that is paid to you for generations to come. When you are satisfied in the bedroom, the fruits come full circle in your home. Your children grow up happy and respectful because you took the time to raise and spend time with them, your wife is happy because you make time to love her both emotionally and physically, and most of all, you are happy when your life is going in a direction that is pleasing to both you and God.

The greatest love you can ever show is to the one you share your bed with. The one you wake up to, rollover with, and most of all, have given your complete self to. The greatest love you can show is the very act of laying down your life for the one you love. Newsflash: as much as the people at the church and on your job so-called love you, neither one of them are willing to take their own life for you.

Asking for sex is not a dilemma when you are willing to give of your own self. I want to ask you something: *if you can't give the person you sleep with every night your absolute best or maybe a better solution to the fix, when will you?*

PRACTICE IT

Some suggestions on starting wholesome conversations about sex with your spouse.

1. Ask your loved one: What do you like or dislike when you are having sex?
2. What would you like me to work on in the natural that would help in the bedroom?
3. Honey, spiritually, what is your picture of me?
4. Sweetheart, what things do I complain about the most that affects our sex life?
5. Tell your spouse about how you really feel when you are naked.
6. Tell your spouse why you don't feel sexy or if you are embarrassed and why.
7. Most importantly, ask your partner to help you fight these bedroom battles starting today.

Chapter Three

Common Misconceptions about Sex

God's gift of sexuality is deeply distorted and many in the church today are deeply wounded in their sexuality. What you watch on TV, what you hear other Christians say, and when you listen to poor sexual experiences, they all play a part in tainting the image of sex in marriage. This image is not only affecting the world, but the church also. Today many believe (even those who are in the body of Christ) some of these lies:

1. "Sex is a bad word."

A. What is sex? Sex is an act, behavior, or activity of any species to reproduce of its own kind. Intimacy, lovemaking, or whatever word you want to put there to make it sound good, still implies *sex!* When you are married, you are free to say this word and hopefully use this word in your bedroom. That is the appropriate place to speak freely about your sex life.

B. God created this act of sexual intercourse as a part of his plan for mankind. In Genesis 1:28, God commands that we are to be "fruitful and multiply; fill the earth." Sex was created by God to refill the earth with his own kind and also for the enjoyment of man. Therefore, as mankind, we have the capacity to enjoy sex and not just need it to only produce as some animals function in this sense. Although the word sex is not mentioned in the Bible, *knew* means the same thing. *Knew,* in Genesis 4:1a: "And Adam *knew*

Eve as his wife," means Adam engaged in sex with Eve and they conceived a son, Cain.

C. It's not wise to talk openly about your sex life in the house around immature children, at work, at school, or wherever you feel it will bring shame to you or someone might misunderstand you. If at any time you are not ready to guard the door you open in talking about sex, don't speak about sex outside your comfort zone, your bedroom. Unless you have an understanding, explain to your children what sex is or is not. If you know exactly what you are talking about regarding sex in a way that would encourage others to wait until they are married, sex is not a bad word. Unwholesome talk about sex is when you downgrade sex in a manner that is not pertinent to reproduction of mankind, boast about the actual act in ways that make others uncomfortable, and most of all spare no detail about the actual act.

D. The enemy has painted such a grotesque picture of sex by flooding the television and world, that any talk outside the bedroom is an inappropriate discussion. Whenever you hear the word sex, because of the way it has been misrepresented, people automatically tell you to hush up. You might actually be receiving information that could bless you or your spouse. In all actuality, sex is probably more important than life itself because without sex, Gods creation could not continue to grow. You need to stop kidding yourself and be open to say this word without conviction but with concern. The only way our world is thriving is because of this one act, sex.

2. "Sex is nasty!"

A. Watching dogs, birds, or any type of animal engage sexually seems funny and almost embarrassing, but that just goes to show how backward our thinking is about sex. You see an animal having sex and say, "Oh my God," but they are being obedient and doing only what has been put in them to do. It is a way of survival for them and a part of the cycle of life for all animal-kind. You need to renew your thinking and embrace what God has ordained as a part of life if you think witnessing an animal having sex is degrading or nasty. This is not to promote bestiality or encouragement to watch animals interact sexually.

B. Promoting pornography is not God's idea of admiring someone carrying out this act, either. Porn is just what it is: the degrading image of what sex is supposed to be about. Porn takes away the privacy and sacredness of an act God has called holy and is to be enjoyed by those in love and married. It is not supposed to be a business or entertainment for others to watch. Throughout the Old Testament, nakedness meant to expose partners, which was disrespectful. In times of old, when a person was exposed as being naked, it was so serious that when Ham saw his dad, Noah, naked, Noah placed a curse on the Canaanites, but not all of Ham's decedents. In the book of Leviticus, uncovering the nakedness of family, friends, sisters, brothers, wives of others, approaching a woman who is unclean, and other acts which allude to porn are simply ways that will defile us as a Christians. In Leviticus 18:26, God declares that, "Ye shall therefore keep my statues and my judgments, and not commit any of these abominations; neither any of your own nations, nor any stranger that sojourned among you." For if you do, you will be cut off.

C. Tell your kids that sex is not nasty but that it is an important part of life. Young adults go through puberty and during this time their bodies are becoming programmed to prepare for a vital role in reproducing. Although talking about sex to your children can be uncomfortable at times, parents have to understand the value of sex first and not shy from what is a part of life for children. But help them to understand the real value of why they are feeling the way they are feeling. This is not the time to run from them and say, "Well, he or she is having wet dreams," or for young girls, "being fast."

D. As a parent, you have experience in having sex; it is better for your children to learn about sex from you than someone who will tell your child whatever and care absolutely nothing about his or her feelings. Sex may be seen as nasty to you, but when you are young and this topic is so taboo, or something you feel cannot be explained, it is not nasty but thrilling in the young mind today. This feeling is normal for all. Sex is not about birds and bees;

it is about life and death. It is about seed sowing and having a continual act that never ends with the one you have been given to in marriage. Parents, if you sow the wrong words now, you will create a mess instead of a masterpiece.

E. How you plant that seed while talking to your children will be critical for the rest of their lives as they begin to embrace the feelings of sexuality. Instead of sowing into the mind of some little horny young man how he is to sow his wild oats, you should be sharing with him the importance of sowing into the right vineyard and watering that garden only. Letting him know that this wonderful act takes place by first having ownership of the garden. To our young men desiring a wife, one thing about a garden in regards to your future wife, whatever you want you can have, you just have to be willing to do the work and plant the right seeds. When you get married, that is your garden, and no man has a right to sow seeds into what rightfully belongs to you. What man would just let someone come and sow seeds in a garden they didn't till and work hard to prepare the seeds for? You will only get out what you put in, and if you are not getting what you planted, whose fault is it? The earth is the Lord's and the fullness thereof and everything that God makes, He makes it good.

F. If you think it's nice to have multiple gardens, try taking care of one. A great example for a young man desiring to have sex is to have him to take care of a garden first. After he takes the time to till, cut, plant, water, and then receive a harvest, he will appreciate the garden he chooses to take care of. Marriage is just like this garden in so many ways and this is why it's important to train your children on this topic. No man wants to invest his hard-earned time to turn around and have the garden utterly refuse to allow him to reap a harvest. Young men, choose wisely and be mindful of the garden you choose to work with for life.

G. Gardening is hard work, but when you have sown, tilled, and laid the foundation with the help of God, it yields fruit some hundredfold, which is filling to the belly.

H. Sex is not nasty; it's a rewarding experience and an emotional opportunity for two people to experience one another in ways no one else ever should.

> *"Let my beloved come into his garden, and eat his pleasant fruits ... I am my beloveds, and my beloved is mine: he feedeth among the lilies ... I am my beloveds, and his desire is towards me"*
> (Song 4:16, 6:3, 7:10).

3. "Sex is not beautiful in the eyes of the Lord."

A. How can something that brings life be nasty, or portrayed as something ungodly? In the eyes of God, it is a beautiful picture, a picture that brings life and not death, an act that produces one of God's own when two married people are joined. In the Song of Solomon, look at how sex is captured: *"Awake, O north wind; and come, thou south; blow upon my garden, that the spices thereof may flow out. Let my beloved come into his garden, and eat his pleasant fruits"* (4:16). *"My beloved is gone down into his garden, to the beds of spices, to feed in the gardens, and to gather lilies"* (6:2).

B. Many people in the body of Christ today feel as if Song of Solomon is a book that is too overrated, let alone sexual. Nevertheless, this book will teach you several things about sex. For one thing, it's God's love for His own people and He is the *l* in love. Who better to write a book about the act of lovemaking? Communicating with your spouse, engaging in foreplay, being ravished and sick in love are all portrayed in this book. While you are running from it, the world is making movies about an act you should already dominate because it is an act which brings our Father glory. Sex, when you are married, *is the opportunity of a lifetime* to be used by God. God's very own power works in us to bring forth a man-child. He didn't leave any instructions; he just said be fruitful and multiply. In other words, just get it done. The instructions on how and what to do during sex he leaves to us with the leading of his Spirit. Psalm 48:14 declares, "For this God is our God forever and ever: he will be our guide even unto death." A lot of people spend so much time wondering who, what, when, where, and why they are doing something a certain way instead of just enjoying each other while working and tilling the garden together. Not only has God given you His Spirit, but you have his mind. Philippians 2:5 says, "Let this mind be in you which was also in Christ Jesus."

C. When you walk in the Spirit, you have several things working on your behalf: God's mind and His leading. So when your husband or wife has the Spirit of God and he or she asks you to have sex in certain ways, do new things, or maybe make love all night, don't quench the Holy Spirit. The same Spirit that tells your husband or wife not to cheat on you is asking you to fill his or her cup and cause it to spill over. Sex is absolutely beautiful in the eyes of God and to abstain from sex during marriage is to come against the very principles our Lord and Savor has put in place. Without this act we would die as a generation, as a people, and as a wonderful opportunity to be like God.

4. "Sex is not the purpose of marriage."

A. **Study 1 Corinthians 7:8–9.**

B. While here on earth, sex is to be enjoyed between a man and a woman, joined in marriage before the Lord, and any other sex outside of marriage is fornication. Sex should never be glorified or even welcomed outside of the marriage arena. Sex should never be the primary reason for marriage, but it should be the purpose in marriage. This world supports all kind of pre-marital sex and this is not the will of God for the child of God. Marriage is where sex is to be found, embraced, and most of all free to partake but of course, this is simple backwards today.

C. Some Christians allow their children to watch sexual acts on TV and this is promoting sex as a casual event that anybody should and can do. The more you welcome the idea of people partaking of it, not being married, and not viewing this act as a sacred time, the more detached the whole act becomes to the purpose of marriage. In these times, sex is so casual and seems so popular to just do, that it is almost impossible to persuade someone that sex is one of the purposes of marriage but it is.

D. In these last days, as the body of Christ, we must continue to promote marriage first, then sex and never vice versa. No, sex will never just keep or become the glue to a marriage but without it, it can frustrate a marriage.

E. I hear so many couples falling in and out of love once they are married but when you wait on the Lord, He brings the wife to the man, and it should never be vice versa. What God brings together, He has to keep together. If a person gets together just for the sake of sex in marriage, when the sex is no longer what it used to be, the marriage will disseminate.

F. When a person says sex is not the purpose of marriage, I have to ask you two questions, *why did you get married and do you not know sex outside of marriage is forbidden by God?* If you wanted love, did you not have that from the Lord, for 1 John 4:16 declares, God is love. Naturally, no one will love you more than your mother and father, but spiritually God is everything we need.

G. As mothers and fathers, we are instructed to allow our sons and daughters to leave our care to go to another dimension of love with their spouse. As much as we love our children, we never stop caring and loving for them, but in marriage the man and his wife become one entity. (see Matthew 19:5)

H. "Therefore, they are no more twain, but one flesh. What therefore God has joined together, (meaning just because you have feeling for someone, doesn't mean that's your wife, God needs to tell you through prayer and not through an illegal engagement like pre martial sex or infactuation), let no man put asunder (see Matthew 19:6)."

I. What is interesting is that no matter how we carried our babies for nine months in the womb, a man needs to get married in order to become one with his wife. It's a beautiful thing how the Lord allows us to bring forth a child. When a man gets married, only then is he joined back to a woman.

J. God is the epitome of love and, remember, God is love. He is our Comforter, Companion, Lover of our souls, and Friend to the end. Okay, let's be very truthful to ourselves. All those things that God can be and is still do not silence the trumpets raging in your physical body, as the need for a companion burns bright.

Hormones are a part of the process God has set in place and they start whether you want to do anything about them or not. As much as you try to fight it off coming into puberty, the feeling to be with the one you say you love seems overwhelming at times. It's not anything that you feel from your mama, grandma, or daddy, but it is a tingling, a tightness, and a sensation that will not go away.

K. No matter how much you try to pray against the feelings or maybe denounce that there is something unique about being in love, you truly desire another person in your life and it is more than just another person to talk to. You want exactly what they have to offer and more. In your mind, the thoughts of them invade your space, time, and feelings. It is something that draws you to them that isn't like the feeling you have for your mom or God. Nope, it is the very feelings God placed inside you to not only be drawn to them, but to desire them sexually—a feeling we all try to make seem like it's shameful to feel.

L. But the emotions, the heat, and the rush that come from the first time you held hands, the chemistry, you knew he or she was the one you wanted for the rest of your life. I believe as married people we forget how crazy we all felt when we first decided we were going to make the person we had feelings for our own. We didn't just want them around like a mother or a brother or a sister in the Lord, we had to have them as something more. We are lying to ourselves when we say we love the inner attributes only, knowing so much of our hormones and emotions are calling to the other person we are attracted to. There is a burning desire to lay with the opposite sex that we all have felt, and that is perfectly normal, if you can be honest with yourself. Looks were a bonus, being spiritual was a must but to say, "I do," to this beautiful creature to make them yours, had to become a reality.

M. That aggressive feeling is what God put in each of us and that is why a male and female united as one desire to become married. All those other blah, blah reasons sound nice, but you could've gotten all of that from the saints, your mom, your teacher, your best friend, your cousins, your dad, and your God—you are married because of sex and that is how God sees fit for you to be ministered to in this way. Sex, the act which you are supposed to get from the one you love, cannot be shared or explained to anyone else close or far. Now, let the church say amen!

5. "Sex should not be discussed in church amongst the saints."

A. Where else are we supposed to find and hear the truth about life while here on earth, if not in the church? I believe churches should set the standard for basic understandings about intimacy and sex. There is a way we can teach the basics of sex without being degrading. Why not teach classes on self-respect, what to look for in a mate, and simple classes on why as a Christian you should wait. Why homosexuality is not approved by God and what is approved by God in relationships. What is the foundation for a good marriage?

B. The reality is that a lot of ministries, can be so out of sync with these areas that they do not know whether to preach this or let parents talk to their own children about it. For this very reason, homosexuality amongst other forbidden sexual sins, are finding their ways into the church. If there is no basis for sexual relationships amongst Christians, there will be no foundation, in which one is to base their relationship on.

C. This whole idea of sex is almost forbidden to speak of in the pews. Words are spirits and what you say you will have. If you have someone in the body of Christ whose marriage is on point, lines up with the Word, and is bearing fruit, then they should have every right to speak freely about having something as beautiful as what they have to the congregation. The older women are instructed to tell the younger women how to be a woman and the same for the older men. Who better to speak on love and sex in church but those whose desire (men and women of good report in marriage) to see the same seed they have birthed out be birthed out in younger marriages?

D. As a matter of fact, we try to be so deep when the whole essence of living and growing in the body of Christ is to make disciples of Christ. If no one is teaching a biblical standard on having a great marriage and how sex should be welcomed, the church will come to an age where birthing out will be obsolete. How can a Pastor explain the important teaching of giving birth naturally to giving birth spiritually, when children don't even understand the whole natural birthing process? In order to even understand spiritual birth, you have to have some awareness of natural birth. Spiritually, something is deposited and likewise in the natural something has to be deposited in order for life to be on board. But if all our kids hear is, sex is bad which is suppose to birth out more God fearing children, what approach do you think they will take when it comes to any other birthing out?

E. In today's society, schools teach sex education and they are simply reading books, not promoting the total being, the whole picture of reproducing after your own kind, or having the blessing of God in your life and family. In schools, sex is misrepresented and talked openly about but nothing that would glorify our Father or create an atmosphere where sex would be welcomed only during marriage.

F. It is vitally important as a body that our children hear the truth, and the truth will make them free. So when they hear sex in any other way—outside of pureness, maturity, and a part of God's plan—they will know the truth and not wonder or laugh about this area. Instead of viewing it as being as big as life itself, it's defined as something everyone is doing and seemingly bad if you are not doing it.

G. As the church, we are beginning to take on the world's view of sex instead of what the Lord has instructed us to do. By not talking about this area as parents, we are all still victims when our children have no understanding and the world raises them up or instructs them on how to grow in this area.

H. SEX, SEX, should be as easy to say as 1,2,3 and when the body of Christ begins to embrace this word as a word created by God, to be used by God, for Gods people, we can take back the real essence of it and bring its sacredness and teachings back to its rightful place; the marriage ministry.

I. Sex, should be discussed in the body of Christ, as a means to promote an overall understanding of its true meaning for human beings who are married.

Chapter Four

What Is All the Fighting About?

"Bill, pay the bills today when you come home. The account information is on the countertop. Okay, honey? Love you, Natalie."

Later that night, Bill gets home and doesn't pay any bills; he's resting and playing video games. On top of getting off late, the children haven't had anything to eat but a snack and the house is nasty. It's Friday and Bill wants to invite some of his friends over to watch the football game again tonight. As a wife, you just want peace and quiet and someone to cook dinner. What could be an easy fix is a complete brawl as the two of you struggle to find out whose needs are more important and why Bill is inviting friends instead of paying bills and figuring out what's for dinner.

Betty hasn't been satisfied for years with Paul because he has problems with himself sexually. He still believes God can heal him; until then, Betty has taken to looking at other avenues for healing outside the church, such as social networking. Every now and then, she finds herself justifying masturbation. In her mind, she's not cheating, just getting a need met that has to be fulfilled. Her friends are in church and support the fact that as long as Betty isn't cheating on Paul, she can attend the "passion" parties and get a few toys for herself. While at work, Betty isn't concerned about the other guys; she has her "silver bullet." It's never crossed her mind to continue praying her husband to be able to satisfy her; years have passed and the desire for sex with Paul is just no longer there anymore.

Cynthia is a prayer warrior. She is the first one in the church and the last one to go home. When she gets home, she wants to pray, but her hubby wants intimacy. They begin to argue and Cynthia goes to pray while Greg goes to the computer. He has a better chance of seeing a video of sex than it happening in his home. He understands God wants him to have his prayers answered, too.

Jordan works all day and comes home just to go to bed. He tries to avoid his wife and the children at all costs, except the oldest daughter. He pays the bills and sees Robin whenever it's necessary. His needs are met elsewhere, so why even talk to Robin? She goes to church and has her church friends; he assumes she has enough conversation there. Two children later, she's a lot bigger and sex is just nasty to him. The visions that go through his mind are definitely not of someone who's big and fat. He doesn't mind sleeping in the guest bedroom since it's routine for him now. He pays the bills, provides for his family, and in his mind is a pretty good father because he is at home and he goes to church every now and then. Robin knows she doesn't work and really has no say so about anything but raising the children, so she doesn't even bother to pursue him or mind him sleeping in the other bedroom. Robin's mind is content as long as Jordan comes home at night and pays the bills.

But Jordan is doing more than paying the bills. He doesn't mind sleeping in the guestroom because he has taken an interest in his own daughter, Janice. She is attractive and becoming more shapely as a young lady now. The more Jordan pushes Robin away, the more he begins to see Janice coming in the picture. So Jordan makes sure to fuss and fight, driving Robin into a hidden shell or to church while he harasses and creeps into his oldest daughter's bedroom. It's been over a year now, and his oldest daughter could be pregnant. Afraid and knowing that her dad takes care of the whole house, she plans to have an abortion and never tell her mom what's been happening while she's away at church. She's a senior now, and as soon as she can, Janice plans to leave this house and her father's tormenting spirit.

Jordan, on the other hand, continues to badmouth Robin for not being a good mom because all she does is go to church. Jordan yells repeatedly to Robin, "You don't work, you're fat, you're ugly, and nobody wants you but the church!" Robin, not standing firmly on what she is declaring, begins crying, calls her church-going friends, and goes out in order to resist being made out as a complete fool in front of the children. Jordan then goes after Janice by sowing into his daughter's mind, "It is me who is paying all the bills, not God, and it is me who is providing for this family, not God, and it is me who you are supposed to be giving yourself to. No man will treat you better than me, I swear, not even God." He tells her every time they are together how he can easily kill her or even bring harm to her mom if she even thinks about saying something. His view of God is that he is God, and he has all the power in this house. Janice continues to believe in the power in him and not in her mom, no matter how much Robin goes to church.

Stephan works all day, goes to church, pays his tithes, and helps everybody that asks him. He is the so-called perfect saint, but when the bedroom doors close, no prayers seem to be answered. He asks God to give his spouse a desire for sex (something, anything), but nothing happens night after night. All day at work, at church, it's like a broken record. The thought of him being able to have great sex with his wife is now played out. Mike tries to combat the thoughts with the Word of God and hanging out with other brothers or sisters from the church, but once he gets home, the feelings of not being able to mount this fine creature are like a boulder sitting on top of him.

There have been so many nights of pain running through his legs. It angers him to know that out of all the women available, the one he has is not helping to suppress these thoughts. He gets up, prays, and takes a warm shower. While the water runs, everything in him is hurting and he can do nothing but plead for God's intervention in this season in his life. *"God, when will this woman I married enjoy having sex again with me when I ask? As much as I do for her and this family, what's wrong with her, Lord? Please help her to get free; I'm hurting too."*

He knows he has a beautiful wife; she just doesn't like sex. So when they do have sex, well, that's what it is. As a matter of fact, he can't recall the last time they were together. Sex is all around, but not in Stephan's home, not like it's supposed to be. In the mind of his spouse, it's a criminal act, something ungodly. At times, the thought of ending it all with his wife have tried to invade his thinking process. He asks God if he is crazy for the way he feels after weeks of going without sex with his spouse. He tries to be strong, but every now and then temptations taste like cold water on a summer day. Satan has begun to whisper, "Go ahead, Stephan; take a sip." Listening but not wanting to listen, he hears the voice saying, "Everybody needs water to live and God will forgive you. Your wife is putting you through all this mess, but you can have almost anybody you want, especially the single lady at the office! As a matter of fact, just tell your wife you don't even have the desire to have sex anymore so she doesn't have to worry about you bugging her!" Satan continues to whisper, "Everything will be all right; trust me."

Thinking he is hearing himself, he begins to unconsciously believe he is hearing from the Lord, not knowing the enemy is setting his plan into action even as he finishes his words with his loved one. *What you lack in marriage is what you will crave for in other relationships that you build.*

Rachel, is a scarred wife, and for her, sex is the last thing on her mind but the first thing her spouse wants, seemingly every day. She pushed everything in front of herself to avoid sex. She argues when there is no need, she hides, and she doesn't find dressing sexy for her mate appealing. She is a great mom to her children, but she possesses the spirit of witchcraft over her mate. How she feels will determine whether or not he will be able to enjoy what belongs to the both of them.

She keeps what she wants and only gives what she feels she needs to when she chooses to. Married but refusing to set aside her own pride or be made whole because of her own way of thinking, no one will be able to touch her completely now that the scar is there. She has deep hurts that have been hidden. Even though she is married and has a relationship with Christ, she refuses to open up and be totally honest with her God and her husband. Every time her husband touches her, she cringes. To be free and never have sex again would be the ideal way of life. To just be married, have children, and make her husband feel so bad that she got hurt that he refuses to bother her about sex is the ultimate plan. The problem with this is that Stacey is clueless about her husband's affair and how all this is affecting him. She doesn't care or even bother to pray for him, but goes on a church fast and prays for others. Her sex life is just not as important as what people see when she is at church.

Michael is waiting on a spouse. At an early age, he became a victim and toyed around with what he had no clue about or knew would become such a powerful feeling. Now he is totally against what God has called natural. Ashamed and hurt, he can never be open and tell how he really feels regarding sex because the enemy has told him nobody would ever understand him. Confused about sex but hiding in the church, he has an unwavering desire to be with the same sex.

Instead of Michael receiving his healing and replacing every unclean thought with war and God's Word, his view of sex is tainted and extremely perverted. He is unaware of how the enemy is causing him to suffer. Sex to Michael is a selfish, feel-good experience for him and his mate instead of being obedient and reproducing after his own kind. This was the commandment spoken by the Lord Jesus Christ. He really does love the Lord so he is still at church, but no one will ever be able to know his real feelings about sex.

If anyone heard his thoughts, or if he told what really happened, many would be hurt and families would possibly split apart. So for now, sex is the way it is.

Pastor Louix has been married for many years and has helped to bring many to the Lord, but when he goes home, sex is nowhere on the agenda. His wife is a wonderful homemaker, but she is not taking care of her body as much as the new choir member with all the drama going on in her life does—and who also needs pastoral counseling. She has lips that drip like honey and the legs of a female track star. There is a lot going on at the church right now and the pastor is praying continually to stay focused, but can't seem to get this woman off his mind. Lacking his own sexual desires and needs being met, he has simply put them on the back burner; all the issues with this woman seem to be receiving more prayer time than the other church members' issues.

His wife is very conservative, but before Pastor Lou got saved, the not so conservative, were the type of women he really preferred. In a constant battle to stay free in this area and to appear not to be going through it himself, he doesn't spend enough time with this wife or bring closure to the needs he has so neglected to take care of. Now, certain thoughts are beginning to become more vivid dreams. Pastor Louix—the highly sought-after example for all mankind, mission-minded pastor, the one who believes he can never fail again (negates he has his own battles to fight and fails to believe lust could be an issue)—mentally believes having sex right now during such a stressful time, with his own wife who isn't as attractive as the new choir member, fails to realize how this whole situation is making him even more vulnerable. Deception in the worse state is deception not perceived.

To the soon to be married, you need your bills paid, the children need food, and you need the feeling of sex in your life. Very lustful now and desperate, you don't mind allowing this so-called fiancé to live with you as long as he helps you pay your tithes and promises to marry you. You are the praying person in church, but your children never see you pray at home. You curse, lie, and insist you are not bad in your own eyes. You say, "The Lord knows your heart." You allow this unchurched sex manic of a man to come into the house and drive you crazy. He promises to marry you, so it's okay that you have sex with him before marriage. The only problem is that when you get through having sex with him and go to bed, he stays up late drinking and gets your younger children out of bed and has sex with both your sons and your daughters. It seems like you are not the only person staying up late burning a candle. In your own selfish desire to be pleased, disobedient, and have sex, you have allowed the enemy to come in and destroy your whole family (eat the whole roll, literally).

To the saved, and sanctified you battle every morning you get up. Just the fact that you woke up presents a problem to the enemy after your marriage. When you get to work, that's a problem; at church, that's a problem; and when you attempt to even talk to your loved ones about the Bible, that's a problem. All the little things, and sometimes the big ones, try to keep you separated as much as the devil can muster. Anything to keep you and your spouse out of agreement Satan sends your way. Although he is unsuccessful in your spiritual walk, he has begun to plant micro seeds in your bedroom. You may not have the problem in the church, at your job, or with other people, but when it comes to the bedroom, one of you engage in sex as a way to make peace with one another. You do a great job appearing to have it all together as a couple, but in the bedroom, the act of sex is carried out but no real intimacy is being built. Sex for you is just something you both do as a couple. For the wife or maybe even the husband, it's not the most wonderful act but atleast you do answer the call when the other person is in need. As long as you fulfill your church and God given responsibilities, going out of your way to get better in the bedroom with your spouse, is considered something only the world would do. In your mind, sex what it is, what is the need to talk about it.

For the religious-minded who are not hearing the voice of God clearly, it's okay if you are not sexually active; besides, you're praying and fasting, right? No! Slowly, you begin to replace this act of sex with one another for other acts of worship outside the home so that eventually, you both lose the desire to have sex all together. You both say, 'Sex is not the most important part of being married." But be not deceived: unless you're dead, the enemy knows what you lack and knows how to wake up or arouse areas in your life you thought were crucified. No, it's not the most important, but it is important. Now, when you go to church you want to seem all deep and not hug the opposite sex; you can't embrace another brother or sister, and this is your excuse for being holy. A young lady who has a man treat her like crap, rape, and abuse her all her life and you cannot even so much as give her a genuine hug without feeling like you have just committed a sin. Why?

There is nothing more embarrassing or outright childish and so unlike God than to see a pastor not able to show compassion to his sheep because he is not receiving compassion at home. It's sad and I truly believe its offensive to those both male and female who may just need the anointing of God to be felt by them. No, you are not supposed to give place to the enemy nor entertain a lustful spirit, but make sure that's what it is when you are not free to show the love of the Father to all men. In these last days, people are looking for the love of God to be evident on and in your life and when you cannot love like Christ, greet with a Holy kiss to your own congregation, you may want to look at how you yourself are being treated at home. Your relationship with your wife is in direct relation to how you will treat those you shepherd.

Whatever your call is in the body of Christ, get it together and walk in the freedom that Christ has called us into. Whether you want to admit it or not, deep down on the inside of the person lacking love at home, there are cravings and lust that must be crucified. Instead of you acknowledging how you really feel and dealing with what God is showing you is in you, you continue to rebuke your own natural feelings that are supposed to be settled with your spouse. Now no member in your church can experience hugs from you and a genuine freedom because you still wrestle with lust every time you are hugged. What's really going on is that what you call lust, when a brother or sister shows a genuine concern and shows compassion for you, is simply the fact that you are the leader of the body. God has called you into ministry and you have a past. And that's exactly what it is, a past. We are new creatures in Christ who are clothed with righteousness. If a hug is going to set you back a few places, are you really called? Now, let the church say amen.

The Enemy

These are sad sex stories in and out of the body of Christ, which is the church, married or not, followed by lust, temptations, fighting, arguing, contentions, hurt, shamefulness, abuse, adultery, molestation, and restlessness. We should expect all of this and more from the world, but we should never expect or give place to any of this in the body of Christ. "What? Know ye not that your body is the temple of the Holy Ghost which is in you, which ye have of God, and ye are not your own? For ye are bought with a price: therefore glorify God in your body, and in your spirit, which are God's" (1 Corinthians 7:19–20).

These are some of the war tactics of the enemy: to rob you (the body of Christ) from having real intimacy and great sex with the mate God has given you, to steal from you your authority and to shame you, to destroy your confession in the sight of God, and most of all, to kill your freedom to be the loving leader and shepherd God wants you to be. It is and will be until the Lord comes back a never ending story for the enemy and his efforts to get us to doubt our power and freedom in God and attempt to make the Lord look like a fool to have picked and placed a promise in us. It may not seem like the devil is around, but he is.

Whether he uses your mind or an individual, don't kid yourself and think he is not present. What so many married, engaged, and in-waiting Christians seem to forget is although the devil was never married, he was in a serious relationship with our Father. Look at some of these amazing facts about the enemy (Isaiah 14:12–23):

1. He was a resident of heaven and knew our Lord and Savior, Jesus Christ, personally.
2. He spent so much time with God that he was actually kicked out of heaven for trying to be like God.
3. He was dressed with all the royalty of heaven.
4. He was the bright day star.
5. He is the great accuser and the father of lies.

6. In the presence of God, he cannot lie.
7. He is so powerful on this earth that without God's Spirit we are sitting ducks.
8. It took the Lord himself coming down in the form of man to overcome sin (the enemy). The Bible says that Satan desires to have us, but because of Jesus' sweat, blood, and tears (our testimony), we can make it through Him only and overcome the devil.

This devil, Satan, was a part of a relationship and held a very powerful position while in the first family. When he was kicked out of the family of heaven, his revenge was geared toward the destruction of all God's creation. *If you think a stalker is bad, welcome to the mind of the enemy. To kid yourself and lack in understanding how the enemy operates in this area of sex is like living with a rotten foot and pretending it's not there. Eventually it will eat the whole body alive.*

His love for you is rage, and his appetite is ravenous for the damnation of souls. He only has one mission in life: to kill, steal, and destroy the very being of Whose we are. Satan hates marriages and especially those that stand for God. He hates the fact that we as saints have taken his place and he will never be able to be a part of this great family ever again. His ultimate goal is to take and destroy as many of God's creation as possible. Can you imagine living in a palace, being entrusted to care for the worship music in heaven, being crowned with all kinds of jewels and gold, then all of a sudden you are ratted out and your true motives are revealed: the plot to try and take over the kingdom. Complete treachery!

If you have never seen or heard of the enemy, let me give you a better picture of who I am talking about. Take that little horror story above and put Satan as the main character and now you can see why he doesn't want you alive or want any part of the reproduction of God's creation to be effective. Satan understands how much God loves his creation and *to be able to stop us from operating as one in marriage would be a direct blow to the plan of God.* If the enemy can drive a wedge between marriages, singles, and those engaged, it would be more beneficial to him because there would be no need to try and kill the babies; just kill the families and they will do it themselves. Put a big boulder between a couple and no one is producing. Make having children so hard that no one wants children.

Jesus Christ loves everything about you except your sinful nature. But in your sinful nature He has given you His nature and expects you to look to Him for guidance concerning your sexual relationships with your spouse. In the body of Christ, you are to seek the wisdom of God concerning your relationships and sober-minded people. 1 Thessalonians 5:17 instructs us to pray without ceasing and that is exactly what you need to do about everything concerning your sex life and the way you feel or see yourself sexually. There is nothing new that anyone can tell God that he has not heard of. There is no situation that is new to Him or unheard of or too embarrassing that He is not willing to listen to.

If you are not satisfying your spouse sexually, take it to the Lord and pray. Ask God to give you strength and speak to your muscles and command them to perform. You are supposed to be a walking example of the Lord and a resident of the Most Holy God; honestly, what part of God is dead or is not able to perform? So when you do perform, you will be able to be exceedingly and abundantly able above all your wife or husband can ever ask for. Command your body as God commanded the valley of the dry bones to wake up from the dead. Where is thy faith, oh faithless generation? Why have you stopped believing and given place to the enemy that your total body is not supposed to be at its absolute best?

Bad sex, good sex, slow sex, tight sex, kinky sex, or whatever you want to call it, when you are having sex, take all those issues and give them to the Father. God is a not a man that He should lie nor the son of man that He should repent, and if He says He wants you to be whole in every area of your life, it is up to you to trust Him and accept Him in making you whole. Stop holding on to years of baggage, pain, regrets, bad sex experiences, or maybe the things that someone has done to you that have given you a sour taste about sex. You are married to Christ first and most of all to the one you say you love. Why keep giving place to the enemy and not fighting for an absolutely great sex life while here on earth?

You complain more than you pray. When was the last time you sat up face to face with Satan and said, "This is my sex organ and it is going to function the way I want it to. In the name of Jesus, Satan, you will not rob, steal, kill, or destroy any part of me. You are an accuser of the brother and everything on my wife or husband is beautiful, so take your accusation and your nasty way of thinking, in the name of Jesus, back to hell with you. I like the way my spouse looks naked; I like every part of his or her body. I am renewing my mind when it comes to seeing it and I respect myself and my spouse. I command you in the name of Jesus Christ to quit trying to defile our bedroom and if I decide to get creative in my bedroom, it's my business. God's Spirit is the conviction and if what my husband and I do doesn't convict our Spirit, you have no place to rob us of our enjoyment while in this bedroom."?

It is written, God has given us creative means and witty suggestion and there are still things as a couple we have not seen. We have a right as a couple to be free in our bedroom because we are temples of the living God and His Spirit is in us. No weapon formed against us shall prosper. Thank You, God, even now as You show me how to praise You for giving me the victory in my bedroom against this devil and the forces of darkness. So if you are really sick of the enemy robbing you of your bedroom glory, begin to shout praises to the Lord, embrace your spouse more when they come in, and vow to each other that you will not allow anything or anyone to come between you both in this holy place.

Anoint your bedroom with prayers and songs from the heart. Tell your spouse how you are willing to make sure this ground is watched at all times and that whenever problems arise in this place, you both will take a revengeful look and make sure that the enemy is not trying to steal what you both have established in this place. There are so many endless battles in the Bible that, because of faith and songs from God's people, God stepped in and gave them the victory. You can have that same victory, just like Joshua and Gideon.

God no longer listens to the music of Satan, but He inhabits your praises when you make a joyful noise to the Lord. He sits up and says, "Listen to my people who are lifting up their voices and praising me." With every song note, heaven rejoices and hell burns with fuel. You have won the heart of God and where His focus was once on the devil, it's all about you. You are the symphony in His ears and the spotlight is on. Have fun in your bedroom and see the devil as an outcast, an old lover, an old jealous ex who wants to be back in your life. You cannot afford to play with the enemy concerning your bedroom and how you react to sex.

In heaven, the enemy was a worship leader who had jewels of every kind to adorn him. He was the music in the Lord's ears, but now the roles have changed. God hears what you are going through, so sing out to worship Him concerning your marriage. Good or bad, you are instructed to make a joyful noise unto the Lord. Wars have ceased and kings were conquered when Gods people opened up their mouths and worshipped the Lord. If the devil can take your song, he can take your joy. If he can take your joy, he will try to take everything. *Now remember, there's a time for everything, so be prayerful and be joyful but make sure you are not unwise and do this before sex.* We will talk more about this in chapter 7.

Lift up your hearts and be joyful today; the King of Glory is listening and waiting for your melodies to be played, right in the middle of your trials in marriage. The enemy has a mission and if you think horror stories are bad, look at the war plan for your marriage concerning the devil. If you are wondering whether or not you should do all of this, wonder no more! If the enemy had his way, your husband or wife would not only cheat, but also bring AIDS into the home and destroy the children by allowing the emotions and stress to drive them into drugs and sex with someone who pays attention to them. His attack is twofold; aim for one and kill two.

It's okay for you to pray sometimes, just be selfish and foolish when you do. Be overwhelmed with life, bills, stress, self, weight, and—good—too many problems. You will not focus on having sex, let along the children? If you don't have them, wonderful! You aren't multiplying. Ultimate plan, get rid of the human race. The devil knows his end and senses he cannot do anything to change it; his plan is to take as many with him as possible. You think roaches multiply, hell enlarges itself daily. Although the devil may have lost his wisdom, like a mad general he has not lost his memories, and definitely still knows what God word says for his people. Make no mistake, the devil remembers what God is capable of for those who love Him and walk upright.

What are you going to do about the enemy who is after your bedroom?

The Fight for Your Life

First rule learned in this book: before learning about war, you must never forget that, no matter what, you will look up to heaven and know you and your spouse are the Lord's responsibility. You don't have the power in you anywhere to change any man or any woman. *Unless the Lord builds the house, you are laboring in vain.* Trying to change your spouse is God's responsibility; you just pray and do whatever God instructs you to do in the Spirit as well as in the natural. It is also critical that you know how to make sure you are remaining teachable and loving to your spouse, as you are the best picture of Christ they will ever see. You both were made for His glory and in His image. In all of God's awesome power and concern for a race, He declares that as His children you are fearfully and wonderfully made. *No matter* what picture the enemy tries to send you of your spouse, don't ever forget who he or she really is.

Weapons will be formed; go ahead and accept that battles will come to your marriage, but no weapon formed against you shall prosper. You may be one of the soft people who have never fought for anything or even felt the need to fight for something, but when the enemy is coming against you and your spouse, you better make up your mind that you are not going anywhere. Claim what rightfully belongs to you and get serious about what God says you are supposed to have. Make your mark right now. Dig your feet in the ground you stand on and declare that as for you and your house, you will serve God with results in all areas of your life, including your sex life. Satan will not have any ground in your home.

You have to confess that you are not crazy, your decision to marry your mate wasn't dumb, you are more than a conquest, you are pleasing, and this land, this house you stand on may be under construction, but it is your home. God has given you this spouse and you are going to get better. Your mind, your emotions, and most of all, your spirit is lining up with the will of God for your life, and you believe that with God nothing is impossible. Confess you are the head and not the tail of your home, and you will continue to walk by faith in order to please God and please your spouse. Know like never before you are the reason your spouse is married; there is no one else and you are the one! Begin to rebuke false thoughts and accusations that there could ever be someone to replace you. Remember, the enemy is the accuser, not you. Rehearse this a couple of times if you have to, but make up your mind that you are going nowhere and your relationship will get better.

You have to understand one thing when you are fighting for ground in your marriage: that you must open your mouth and make confessions daily. So get motivated and open your mouth. In the Bible, they didn't just spend a few minutes here and there confessing, it was hours and sometimes days. Don't hold anything back; get desperate and realize that if you really want to see results in your marriage, it's not so much that it's you fighting, but you are using the power of your words to begin setting the atmosphere for God to do what your words are commanding of Him. The Bible declares you are to command God by opening your mouth. "Command ye me, saith the Lord." Our fight as spiritual people is spiritual, and any battle that is to be won must be overcome in the Spirit first. Open your mouth.

You do a great job speaking life into everyone else, but how about speaking life into your own bedroom?

Battles are going to come and trials, too, but God is demanding that as married couples you stand your ground and refuse to allow anything to overtake you by using the power of God. What looks really bad today is just preparation for greater days ahead. If you don't learn how to fight for the small things in your marriage, you can forget fighting for bigger things that are sure to come. The best is yet to come, but if you are a wimp, get mad, and run every time Satan throws blows at you, you will never see the brighter days in your sex life or your marriage.

How many times have you heard this saying: "the battle is not yours, it's the Lord's"? Then declare to the devil with God's Word, that "I will bless the Lord at all times and His praise shall continually be in my mouth!" Yeah, it's the Lord, but you still have to show up. So the enemy is going to bring the trials, but you don't have to give place to the devil. Send his tactics and poison back to him by praising God for being blessed with a spouse.

Like the Hiroshima bomb, the devil comes to wipe out the human race and the very thought of godly marriage. Whether you want to fight for your marriage or not, remember that if it's worth having, it's worth fighting for. In America, although we have wars and soldiers have to leave, we will never stop defending this great country. How much more will you as the people of God continue to fight and defend what belongs to you? Each family born represents first families, but the devil's plan is to make sure you are the last of your kind. This is a fight whether you want to call it one or not and whether you want to fight fair or not; when you stand back and watch or think Satan doesn't exist, you will lose every time. But when you put on the whole armor of God, open your mouth, walk by faith, and declare what rightfully belongs to you the way it's supposed to, heaven hears and God answers.

Practice It:

Confess this right now while walking all around your bedroom!

1. All power is given unto me and I shall have what I say if I believe according to the Word of God! God has given us everything that pertianeth to life and death, therefore whatever we lack sexually as well as naturally, we can obtain.
2. My body is made whole, my life is being led by God, and I shall possess what belongs to me. I shall have a great sex life. I shall have a creative mind for this unique area in my marriage.
3. I shall see the fruits of my labor and I shall learn how to give love as well as receive it. I am a loving person and I have the power to make passionate love to this man or woman and enjoy my spouse for the rest of my life. I expect my bedroom to be a place of healing, restoration, excitement, and peace.
4. I am in control of my emotions and feelings today. No other picture will I entertain but my wife or husband because my eyes are fixed on my spouse.
5. I am your righteousness and every part of me shall be made whole from the top of my head to the soles of my feet. From my inside out.
6. I am a virtuous woman and I am a man of favor.
7. My season of great intimacy and sex is upon me even now, because my season of prosperity is in my mouth and upon me even now.
8. I will be able to embrace and show compassion toward all my sheep in which the Lord has entrusted me with. I am free in my mind and free in my soul when I show godly love toward the opposite sex.

Chapter Five

What Does Satan Want from Me? What Is His Strategy in My Marriage?

Annihilate you!
Blindside you!
Control your confession!
Deceive and defile you!

Tactic 1: ANNIHILATION

> *The thief cometh not, but for to steal, and to kill, and to destroy: I am come that they might have life, and that they might have it abundantly.*
> John 10:10

    Annihilation is the complete destruction of something. John 10:10 clearly states how the enemy desires to steal, kill, and ultimately destroy the human race. Too many people, even Christians, take the enemy as a joke and not a real threat in marriage. Many fail to understand that Satan is not the bill collector, one whom you can just run games on, pay when you have the money, make a mess out of what you borrowed, and then when you get ready, decide you are ready to fix your situation. *No way*; he is the repossession devil. Whether you have the money or not, he will never stop bothering you if you leave any doors open in your marriage. When you sin, if you are not praying for God's forgiveness and turning from your wicked ways, he is allowed to come and collect what is due. The devil knows the wages of sin is death. You may run, but you will never hide your sins from the enemy. Praise God that He has the forgiving power over the enemy, that once we confess our sins, they are put in the sea of forgetfulness.

God is your intercessor, credit fixer, and most of all, shield. He is your power and strength from this devil. When you are faithful, honest, humble, and admit your faults, He is faithful and just to forgive you of your sins. He understands your shortcomings and continues to ask you to come and reason with Him. As big as God is, He is saying let us reason together. Come on, even God understands you are not perfect and that you will make mistakes. It is important to take your case to the Lord before things get really out of control. Jesus Christ wants to be a part of the mistakes in your life beforehand, so that your file will not be sent to the bill collector, the repo man, the devil. *It is the devil's ultimate goal to rid you and your total family from the face of this earth.* But God has come to bring us life and total freedom in every area of our lives.

It is a promise to all creation that trials and tribulations are going to come, but God will lift up a standard up against the enemy when we are in right standing with Him and ask for forgiveness. As you pray, communicate with your spouse about life, attractions, lusts, temptations, dislikes, and how you both can get better; only then can you look for the results in your marriage. You'll never see growth if you don't know where you are. Satan is not smart, he only plans and plays off the fuel we give him. When we argue and fight against one another, we are only helping in the enemy's plan.

He doesn't have to do much if you and your spouse are always at each other's throats and never pray together. If one person cares more about sex than the other, this can become an issue. If one prays and the other doesn't, that's a problem. If one disciplines and the other one doesn't, that's a problem. These little problems go unsolved everyday in Christian lives, but eventually are brought back full circle as they become incorporated into the grand scheme of the enemy. On the flipside, if you are praying but you aren't growing together in word and deed, you will always lack the power God has given you as a couple.

When it comes time to fight and defeat the enemy, because you both are at each other's throats, there is no defending your home. Neither your house nor family will be able to stand.

You owe it to yourself and your spouse to make sure you are honest with one another and to leave no topic left undone as the Lord leads you to release your diary. Although this is a process, it is one sure way of being able to walk in your God-given authority; by yielding to God and your spouse and at the same time, you will begin to grow in all areas of marriage. What you hide will come to the light whether it is good or bad. The Bible is filled with people trying to hide their imperfections only to have them manifest later.

As a people who have a relationship with God, we don't have to wait to be deceived about anything. We have everything we need that will help us to defeat this enemy who comes to pick up the scraps of our marriages. So if you think fussing, abstaining from sex for no reason, finding fault, blaming, and most of all, lusting are mere scraps, you are so wrong. The enemy uses these scraps which mean nothing to you to slowly steal, kill, and destroy the very plan God is trying to place in your life. There is no such thing as "this is just the way it is;" that is a lie. If you spend all your day fussing and trying to make arguments to keep from spending time with each other, it is just a matter of time before you will not have one another, God forbid. If you don't know, all you have to do is ask. If you have not in your marriage, it is because you are asking the wrong person. You need to ask the One who is actually able to help you and not be deceived in your marriage.

If you are married and you have never read the Bible, close this book up now and go read it. You will never gain any wisdom from this book without first understanding the Word of God. This book provides practical instruction on how to fight and be victorious in the sex life of your marriage. Not being prepared spiritually will only bring *annihilation* from the devil. Before you can fight in any battle, you are going to have to learn about your weapons.

What are they? The Holy Bible is packed with weapons of warfare that will prepare you for both the spiritual and the natural side of living. It tells us from beginning to end to dwell with your spouse according to knowledge. That knowledge is not just head knowledge, but the knowledge that comes from spending time with Jesus to show you some of the mysteries about your better half. Just to name a few of the weapons we have may look little to us, but they are mighty through God: ones testimony, praising God, praying, fasting, having faith, knowing God's Word, the breastplate of righteousness, and simply standing on your confession of faith.

If you have read your Bible and have some knowledge of God and how he operates, welcome to the rest of the enemy's tactics, numbers 2–4. I like to refer to this part of the book as "Combat Marriage Class 101." Here you will need *faith, love, and the Word of God*. The enemy is going to come, but he will not be able to destroy you because God has promised that although the weapons are formed, no weapon formed against you shall prosper. Satan has no more power over death, nor can he annihilate a child of God unless we are ignorant of his devices and give place to the enemy.

Tactic 2: BLINDSIDE YOU

> *There is a way that seemeth right unto a man; but the end thereof are the ways of death.*
> Proverbs 16:25

What does it mean to be *blindsided?* It means attacking somebody suddenly, hitting the person on a side where his or her peripheral vision is obstructed. Whether you want to fight or not or whether you believe there is a devil or not doesn't negate the fact that he is not going to stop coming against you or your spouse. You hear a lot of times that the battle is not ours, but we can never forget that we do have a part to play in the battle. Since God said there is a battle going on, we have someone to fight against. Here is the devil's second war room strategy: to blindside you in your sex life.

When you miss this concept, problems will surely come. God has come so that you would have life and a life of abundance. The devil has come so that you would be afraid, stolen, ungrateful, destroyed, and dead in your marriage. God comes that you would wake up in love, thankful for your spouse, and ready to live with him or her through it all. Satan comes that you would be dead in your homes, unaware of your daily acts, stolen from your spouses due to the cares of this world, destroyed in your thinking, and dying each day that you stay in a miserable marriage. You want a divorce, but you say it's wrong when you have already mentally signed the papers years ago.

Everyday is a fight for you just living with your spouse; you focus all your attention on one area so that you never see what God is actually doing in your life or your spouse's life. You may be the one who makes a big deal out of nothing and this is exactly what the enemy wants. You refuse to engage in sex with your spouse and you put up every excuse. You say you are free, and truly you are, you just have become so blind that you have failed to see how the enemy is using you to put chains on your spouse. It's all about you: how you want life to be, whether you are happy or things aren't going your way, if life just shines on you. But in all actuality, your life is but a vapor—here today and gone tomorrow.

You haven't learned how to take all those wiles from the enemy (which are simply uncontrolled emotions and temper tantrums not taken to God). You haven't learned that being married is not about you but the three of you: God, you, and then your spouse.

You are blindsided when you are not able to see how the Lord is using trials and tribulations in your home to get you to depend on Him and not yourself. Frustrations come when things don't go according to your plans, which is a direct indication that you are blindsided. Although you are one flesh, you are still two different people who have needs and whose spirits are required to be daily in the presence of God. You may be married and sex is not all it's cracked up to be, but I wonder where your real focus is. Could it be that God is giving you a dose of your own medicine? *When you don't spend time with God, sow into Him, sacrifice for Him, cry out to Him, and most of all, love on Him, could it be possible that you are reaping what you are not giving God?*

Then you turn around and expect your spouse to treat you the way you should be treated! Why? As long as the earth remaineth, you are instructed to sow in order to reap. We serve a jealous God, one that requires maintenance in loving Him even more than our spouses. If you want really great sex, I dare you to go after God like you are going out of your mind. While you are there in the presence of God, ask him to open your eyes on how you minister to Him and most of all, to your spouse. Ask God to be able to see as He does concerning your spouse, especially when you are intimate. When you take care of His business, what you believe Him for, even if it's great sex you desire, God is no respecter of persons and he is a rewarder of those who diligently seek after Him. He will give you your heart's desires only after making sure He has your heart. Believe me when I say that God will make everything work for your good, just try Him. It is a lie from hell to believe Christian marriages cannot be on fire for God and one another. You want the desires of your heart, "Seek ye first the kingdom of God and his righteousness and all these things will be added unto you" (Matthew 6:33).

Being married is for the procreation of human beings and the mere enjoyment of human life with one another to replenish the earth. Sex is one of God's greatest gifts to human kind. When it comes to being happy, pleased, and full of joy, you must know that only comes from God. "Every good gift and every perfect gift is from above" (James 1:17a). If you are unhappy in your marriage, how is your relationship with Christ and where are you looking for the answers? When you depend on your spouse to put a smile on your face, you are blind; you should wake up every day already with a smile because of the One smiling on the inside of you. When things go wrong, and they will while you are married, learn to look to God first before you lose your composure or look at your spouse as the reason.

When you are blindsided, you tend to look one way and maybe just focus on all the bad or what you think you have to have in marriage. But remember to always look at the bigger picture. What you don't see is what you usually miss out the most on instead of focusing on what you do see. So sex is not great now, but you are married and it can get better. So you have no intimacy, but you do have one spouse, someone who is willing to get better and hopefully to listen also. You will have to learn to stop focusing on what is going wrong and put some of your positive energy on what's going right. You know the old saying, "The grass is greener on the other side"? That's a lie. Here is why: as long as there is work to be done on your end, it always looks like something is better when there is lack on your part. But I bet you had no idea how much hard work went into keeping that grass green on the other side!

See, you want some instant grass, no problems, and quick results? You can tell yourself all day that you can get that, but that grass usually doesn't stay around long and doesn't endure harsh weather. It's fragile, but the grass that you have to fertilize in season, water, cut, and keep trimmed is the grass that comes back every season for being good to it. Quit coveting other people's results and make your own results. We are Christians and we have what we say. If you don't take the time to sow into your bedroom: tilling, watering, speaking life, being creative, not being boring, not complaining, submitting, and most of all, keeping your bedroom in prayer, you will always believe the grass is greener on the other side. You shall reap a harvest in your bedroom if you are faithful and not faint, but sow into yourself and take the blinders off your eyes.

One of the biggest problems that Satan had while living in heaven was becoming blindsided himself. He wanted more and he wanted to be like God. It was not enough that he was living with God and called the day star; he wanted more. He believed the grass was greener on the other side and he was the grass. Being blindsided always causes one to focus more on one thing instead of what is really going on in and around them.

It's sad to see couples who don't realize what they have and it takes other couples telling them just how good they have it. Have you ever wondered where that spirit came from? Lucifer. He had it so good in heaven but was too greedy and blinded by his own lust to see just how good he already had it and he wanted more. The same lust and prideful view that led to his destruction he tries to use in every marriage to get a blindsided spouse to think, it's not me, it's my spouse.

The Blinders: You

There are countless Christians settling for divorce today. Many never come to know how they are still married to the problem: themselves. Instead of giving themselves wholly to the Lord, they continue to contend with God and give place to the devil. Some never come to realize that God is trying to do a new thing inside of them and when they fight against Him, He's not able to help them. So they may win in the outward fight as problems come to their home; they see them and handle them. But when it's about self, it's a whole different battle. One in which you have still not learned to be successful in. So you get your annulment, but have you ever divorced yourself?

When our spouses have the anointing of God in their lives and they try to correct us in love, we have to find it in our hearts to know they only want what's best for us. It's not that he/she is supposed to be better than you or to have a competitive spirit in marriage, but to have a coming together to sharpen one another. We can take correction and blows by everyone except those we love. It can even be the same word given by the Lord and still mean nothing until we hear it from someone else. Isn't it ironic that you are healing and teaching others how to love and you can't teach and love at home? Or your family is not receptive when you correct them? Of course it hurts for the one you love to correct you, but they have no vindictive motives in telling you the truth. Not only do they represent Christ, they represent you.

The Blinders: Your Spouse

So the other person begs and hounds you for sex all the time; you can hardly sleep without the constant attack of begging. What do you do? Roll over and ask your spouse very nicely, "Honey, have you ever thought that instead of always hounding me for sex that this could be the time that God desires for you to begin to pray for me and my body? Honey, do you realize that I love you and enjoy you, but can you spend some time, please, just praying over me? Praying over my body, over my mind, my legs, my head, my pains, and all that brings you joy? Can you help me to maintain what is yours and what you so dearly love?"

This is the perfect time to make it a reality that sex is just not about the midsection and what you can do in bed, but about all the things that you love about each other. Having sex is absolutely wonderful, but what about all the other things that make a person wonderful and make you feel good? When is the last time you said something about that? This is the time to help your spouse see the blind condition in his or her life. Encourage your spouse on how you love their desire for your body because you never want them to stop longing after you. Tell them, "Thank you for loving what you have chosen in a wife/husband, and I love that you hunger for this garden, but even a garden needs a period of rest. But, baby, please don't come to this garden to partake, sweetheart." Always build up your spouse before you just say no, leave an expectation in your no.

It's healthy, as well as playful, for your spouse to desire you in such a way that it causes them to long after you. What isn't healthy is when a man in a marriage no longer desires his wife. For many men in marriages of this kind, where the desire is gone for whatever reason, healing seems almost impossible. But with God all things can be restored and put back into the right perspective. Never say no without giving a next time! Very gently, tell your spouse not to be blinded by what's between your legs only, but ask him or her to be sensitive to the times that God is using you to intercede for your body and the jewels you have. Remind your partner that, as much as you love each other, you need to know he or she cares for and desires the rest of you, too. Inform your spouse how the Lord can use him or her right now in the middle of the night to minister to your body and soul.

Men have muscles that need to be massaged and worked between their legs, and if you want to be able to enjoy a muscle and make sure it's strong all the days of your life, work the muscle. Muscles have to be exercised and built up in order to endure and stand when weight or pressure is applied. For women, it's the same thing; we have to learn to appreciate how delicate our bodies are, but realize our organs are made to operate with a male. The more you practice, learn about your body, and pray for your insides as well as your outsides the more you will appreciate the harmony you both can experience while making love.

I personally know that after babies, women deal with all kind of hurts and pains during sex. Then you have some people who simply don't understand the makeup of the body and so you have to communicate. You have to say when things just make you uncomfortable, without fussing, but continue to have a willing heart to want to learn how to get better.

Most pains and aches take place at night and I believe it's because the body is at a state of rest finally from the day. When the Bible says weeping may endure for a night and joy comes in the morning, this is definitely a true saying. This is a good time not to complain about your body, but to invite your spouse to know about that other parts of your body need a healing touch as well. Take comfort and believe in your partner for what he or she is able to do besides wake you up for sex. Ask the one that's up to rub you down since he or she isn't sleepy.

Tell your spouse why you would like to have sex if this or that was not hurting, but never complain or make it seem as if you are just never interested in the person. That opens all kinds of doors for the enemy. Remind him or her again to touch you in a way that would not only feel good for him or her, but for you, too. Some of my most romantic nights have been the nights I have said no to sex, only to tell Walter yes to back rubs, cuddling, and reading together because my knee was really painful. Walter knew then that other things needed healing and without even asking, he was already up praying, getting pain medicine for my knee, helping to elevate my knee while it was swollen, and making me comfortable. After all those things were in place and later in the middle of the night, the pain went away, and the Lord woke me up to remind me that; it would be a great idea for me to wake my husband up, and minster unto him.

We have to believe we are helpers one to another and the same way a woman can make a man feel wonderful, a man can make a woman feel exhilarated by ministering to her emotional needs before sex. If you never speak on why you absolutely don't want to have sex, you have become blinded—you don't want your spouse to be able to "see" what's really going on. If you just don't want to make love, ask your spouse to help you. But whatever you do, don't get mad and just outright refuse sex; open up your mouth and speak on what's really bothering you. Learn to capitalize on moments like this that your spouse is up and you have her full attention. You will be surprised how these spontaneous and or random moments can become the best nights of your life.

Finally, to the ones who blame their spouses for simply just not feeling the way they do about sex, I hear you. But listen to your spouses and see why they don't enjoy sex as much as you. If you love the way they make you feel, why don't they love the way you make them feel? Put your pride under the bed and listen. It may take a couple of hours of foreplay or talking before lovemaking, but most of all, you have to be willing to incorporate your spouse into this act so you both look forward to it. Encourage your spouse throughout the day with hugs, kisses, simple acts of kindness, helping in the house, and most of all, by setting the atmosphere. It's your house; if you want a night of passionate love, it has to start the time you wake up and last throughout the day. Midnight doesn't mean microwave, but it means ministry. God has equipped you with all the things you need to rule your home as well as your spirit. You want great sex? Start by waking up and declaring it! You have what you say.

Tactic 3: CONTROL YOUR CONFESSION

"Death and life are in the power of the tongue: and they that love it shall eat the fruit thereof."
Proverbs 18:21

One of the biggest mistakes Eve made was talking to the devil without getting an understanding from the Lord. Eve thought, just like some of us assume, that she had been there before and knew what to say or do concerning this area. We think there is no need to be spiritual and ask God about sex. Wrong answer! As Christians, we can learn a lesson from Eve and our Savior, simply to use the Word of God on the enemy in every area of our lives, with an understanding. If a question arises in your mind that causes any doubt or needs careful consideration and a confession must be made, that is the time to get on your knees and seek God for guidance before you come to any final conclusion.

Proverbs 4:7 (emphasis mine) declares, *"Wisdom is the principal thing; therefore get wisdom: and with all thy getting get understanding."* Please make no mistake and think that just because you quote the Scripture that it is going to be enough because the enemy knows the Bible back and front, too. You are going to have to live what you say. The enemy, Satan, doesn't have the wisdom of God, but he has the understanding on how we operate as human beings. He has had all of history to learn, but still has no knowledge of how God operates when He controls our lives. The power in making confessions and seeing results comes from dealing with the enemy with knowledge, having faith in the Word of God, and walking not in your own understanding, but leaning on the understanding of the Lord.

Now let me make this point clear: you cannot just use the Word of God on the enemy because of what you heard the pastor say or what you heard someone on TV say. The words you are to use that will bring forth power are the words that you release by speaking with an understanding and prayer. This is why it's vital that in all you're reading to get an understanding. When situations come up in your marriage, go to the Word and God in prayer. Who cares that you have been here before and that you have been praying? My question to you is, have the results manifested yet? Keep praying and keep speaking. Also, you must begin to meditate daily on Scriptures in the Bible that deal specifically with the issue at hand.

If the devil can get you speaking in the times when it is best that you be quiet, he has achieved one of his goals. He understands the law of God which says you shall have what you say, but sometimes we simply forget this powerful phrase. Proverbs 17:27 declares that "he that hath knowledge spareth his words: and a man of understanding is of an excellent spirit. Even a fool, when he holdeth his peace, is counted wise: and he that shutteth his lips is esteemed a man of understanding."

We can recall the incident in the Bible where the disciples could not cast out certain demons and they asked Jesus why. Jesus responded that "this kind cometh out by fasting and prayer." Why? When you are fasting you are leaning not to your own understanding and ability, but on total dependence of the Word of God to operate on your behalf. I wonder just how many Christians today fast concerning situations that seem threatening to their marriages or when something is simply beyond their own human ability. But when you fast and pray, you deny yourself and put God at the forefront. It is absolutely none of you and all of His Spirit. Even Jesus knew that in order to be able to resist the enemy in his trial that lasted forty days, he needed to refrain from eating to be able to walk and have total dependence on the Holy Spirit.

Far too many Christians have become ignorant of the devil's devices and are simply unaware of the tools we have to defeat this enemy. You go to church, pray, and fast about everything concerning the church and come home and there is no fire to be found. How many married couples today in the body of Christ have ever fasted or only fast as the church fasts? As a matter of fact, when was the last time you have fasted just as a family?

Therefore, some have never experienced the deliverance that comes from giving yourself totally to God so that He is able to move on your behalf concerning your marriage, children, or life when you speak. What about praying? Did Jesus not say that these kinds also go out by praying? Look at this: every day in Genesis, Jesus met Adam and Eve in the cool of the day for fellowship. Why didn't Eve take what the devil offered her to Jesus then? I could even imagine her saying, "Lord, the serpent told me this, what do you have to say because I would like to be more like you. What do you think?" Or, why didn't Eve turn to her hubby and ask, "Honey, what do you think or should we even go ask God?"

Why not? She assumed she had been to church, heard, and understood what she wanted to hear, but it wasn't clear in her heart or even in Adam's. He sat there and did not speak with wisdom or an understanding. So when she went to speak or confess God's words, the enemy played on her lack of understanding and own lust. She hadn't fully gotten an understanding on what she heard, but she heard. Instead of going to commune with Adam or the Lord, she perceived that what she wanted and what she heard were right in her own eyes without the say of the Father.

Now, fast forward to today and how many of us as married couples are still guilty of this sin of self-gratification? Even in using God's Word, we justify what we want and never ask God about what is best for us. Another valid point is that anything you have to sneak and say or do is always bad. If you feel guilty talking to the Lord about it, that should be an indication that you really need to ask God about it before you respond. Make no mistake about it, you must go and ask God about even the most embarrassing of situations and never think He doesn't care, because he does.

As embarrassing as this is, I have to share this story because I believe this will bless many of you who read this part on confessing. I remember having my first son and everyone telling me that a lot of times when a woman has a child, she later has to suffer with hemorrhoids. Well, I didn't know a lot about them, other than they are not good to have.

I did not want hemorrhoids and refused to believe I would ever have to deal with them. I remember taking this accusation to the Lord and asking for understanding. I even went and looked all over the Bible to see if this was just something I was supposed to accept since I was having a baby.

Low and behold, after praying and hunting all over the Bible, I found it. The name was not literally hemorrhoids in the Bible, but *emerods.* In Deuteronomy 28:27, it was a curse put on those who would be disobedient. I went down on my knees and began to pray and ask God to make sure I never get these and every day that I was pregnant I would confess I was his righteousness and I did not have to receive hemorrhoids or emerods in any form. I have since had three children and have never dealt with hemorrhoids from any child.

I studied and got an understanding on what it is I am supposed to receive and not receive according to the Word of God. If you have ever dealt with this curse and still do, read about this in 1 Samuel 5:6–9 and Deuteronomy 28:27 and rebuke the enemy concerning this area to receive your freedom. Make a confession daily that you are the righteousness of God and you are not cursed. You do not have to receive these either. You have the Word and the Word has come to make you free.

God will not hide anything from you when you ask. But if you do not ask, you will never know. So why when you make a decision and begin to speak haven't you taken the time to talk with God about it? Do you still honestly think you are getting away with anything by not asking? What grown human being still acts like a child and deceives his or her own self?

This simple but very costly confession and communication with the enemy shows us how we are all very vulnerable when we are unlearned in the Word and make the wrong confessions out of the abundance of our hearts. Every Christian should use this story of Eve and the enemy as a learning guide to study in order to show oneself approved unto God so that when you rebuke the enemy or make confession, you know exactly what you are talking about. It is a shame and simply an embarrassment to take what you think you heard or have heard someone say whether in church or on TV and try to use it on the enemy. Unless you know what you are talking about and you have the authority from God after praying about the situation, to say what thus saith the Lord, you should hold your peace and continue to commune with the Father in prayer.

When you pray about a situation that is troubling, especially concerning your sex life, God will give you the answer and peace about that which is causing a great strain on your marriage. It is a promise from God that if you cast your cares on Him, He will care for you and help you. He also instructs you to come to Him and reason about whatever it is that you have going on before you make final decisions about anything. Even something like not having sex with your spouse needs to be discussed with the Father (and your spouse). In everything you say and do, you must make sure to guard your heart and walk in unison with the Word of God for your life. There are many ways and devices in a man's heart. We need the Lord to give us His heart, because our hearts are desperately wicked. Without the heart of God leading and guiding what you say and do, you will live a life based on your own misguided decisions.

If you want to be able to make a positive confession, get in the Word and pray about what your heart is saying. Make sure every word lines up with God's Spirit. God is talking loud and clear in these last days, especially where trouble reigns in your home. It is not His will for you to have a house that is divided in any shape, form, or fashion. He is the great peacekeeper and more than anything desires that you speak what He says and have what you say. My son and daughter in marriage, you must know when confession is made to have faith, pray, fast, and guard your heart and you shall have what you say. 1 John 5:14 says, "And this is the confidence that we have in him, that, if we ask any thing according to his will, he hearth us; and if we know that he hear us, whatsoever we ask, we know that we have the petitions that we desired of him."

Walter and I have been married over ten years now and it has not always been as beautiful as it seems, but it has definitely been all we have spoken and more. I remember the time we were still learning how to confess the Word of God in our lives. It was hard at times, as what we confessed did not always manifest right away, but thank God we didn't throw in the towel on one another or give up. After confessing for years that I would have a son, two years later into our marriage my first son, Walter Jr., came.

Then we wanted him to have a playmate, but it had to be a boy. We started confessing and began to name this second child as soon as possible. Nine months later, a male child was born, William Princeton Kirkland. Finally, I thought a girl would be nice to have. We got on our knees and started praying for a girl and then we asked God to give us her name. Later on, we went to the doctor and they swore up and down it was a boy. We refused to believe it. I went home crying and still confessing that we had heard God and this was our daughter in spite of the doctor's report. Every day we would call out her name, Elisabeth, regardless of what others said. We knew what we had prayed for and what we desired from the Lord.

People had their doubts when I told them it was a girl and that I was confessing like I did with my boys, even some people in the church did not believe me. But because we serve a God who gives us our hearts' desires when we are obedient and line up with His will, nine months later it was a beautiful girl we called Elisabeth Rose Kirkland. I totally believe that in order to please God you must exercise your faith by standing on what you are confessing in God. I believe a lot of people in the body of Christ today have lost their control in their confession. They want to speak life, but it's so hard. They want to say nice things and believe God for a change concerning their spouses, but they haven't got the faith or patience to believe God for what they are asking. The enemy has come in and sown the seeds of doubt and unbelief that to stay in a marriage and wait for change seems unbearable.

When was the last time you balled up your fist and began to confess that you have what God has promised you? In spite of what stuff looks like, in spite of what you don't have, what are you saying? When was the last time you fasted and prayed to see change in your own life or for your spouse or maybe even for the children? Maybe even for the bank account or for your sex life? When was the last time you even fasted from sex and prayed the whole time you were away? When was the last time you prayed about something you really desired? After you prayed, what was your confession? How long did you confess and pray?

Did you get into position for the blessing? Do you really want what you are praying for and confessing or you just saying mere words? When what you are praying for doesn't show up, are you back to whining and complaining? So what if you aren't able to have sex tonight with your spouse, this could very well be a chance for you to put seeds in the ground through prayer concerning this area. Instead of complaining or refusing to show love in other ways every time you are not able to have sex, how about now you begin to bless God in that you are not ruled by your emotions and can say, "Honey, I still love you and even though we are not having sex tonight, I am so glad we are married. We have an awesome marriage and I know our sex life is wonderful because you are so incredible and I love how you make me feel. But goodnight and go to bed!"

Remember, you shall have what you say, death and life lie in your tongue, so what are you saying? Don't go to bed mean and spiteful, but go to bed speaking what you want. Speak those things which be not as though they were. Confess this now: the sex in my marriage is hot as fire; yes, my spouse is wonderful; yes, I have enough sex that my cup runneth over; and yes, I am pleased with the wife or husband of my youth. Quit speaking death every time you cannot get your way. Remember you have not because you ask not and when you ask, you have asked without understanding and faith. Change your confession in your bedroom and believe you have what you say. Prophesy to yourself. What Christian doesn't profess over his own life? We have the power to create whatever we desire as long as it lines up with the Word of God. Start confessing.

Don't you know that it is the confident woman who has what she says and walks in her field of fruit? There is nothing more powerful than seeing a confident woman in the Lord. For this very fact, her husband rises up and calls her blessed because she has learned to study to show herself approved unto God. This is not the woman who watches TV all day because she is too busy getting prepared to be at peace when the man of God comes home.

Her focus in not on her or his lack, but on the promises of God, and she knows what those promises are. She spends her nights praying and making sure he is completely satisfied. She is the woman who uplifts and encourages her man. She is the woman who fasts for herself and her family without a church mandate. She is the woman who desires to please her husband, so she asks him what it is he wants. She is the woman who desires that they both talk during, before, and after sex. She is the woman who says her husband is the man of this house and he has his way; she knows how to speak and be quiet at the same time. She is the woman who well rules her spirit and her home. She understands and makes full proof of her calling. She is the woman that has created exactly what is already hers. She understands submission because as her husband asks, she responds out of love and respect for the body of Christ in him. She understands it's not him asking, but his request comes from the same God inside her. The Holy Bible declares that we are not our own; we were bought with a precious price.

This is the woman that cannot be deceived because she has made it her business to know that what God has put together no man can put apart. She understands firsthand even after years of marriage that this is a work in progress and that you have what you say. She understands that trials and tribulations are going to come, but she is willing to work them out as a team. She understands she has a battle buddy for life both spiritually and naturally and to tear him down would be a direct and terrorist thing to do to her own home. This is a woman of faith and confidence in God and not man.

Son of God he is. A man of understanding and sensitive at the same time to his wife's calling. A man who is learned in the Word, but humble, too. He is not stupid about the world around, but sound in his decisions. A man who is free in his own marriage, but balanced enough to show the love of God to others in the body. His hugs are genuine, as he gets them from his wife all the time. She is the apple of his eye and no other woman can replace what he sees. His flaws are made known to her and she hides them in her heart and prays fervently about them to God. He sees his weaknesses and professes his new strengths in the Lord. He speaks with authority and has never stopped learning from the God within both of them.

He has his place as king and lord of his home, but understands his leadership role is that of a father with love for his children. His first concern is God and that that picture is shown as he raises his own flock up in the Word. He is the example of the priest, and all the children respect his hand of authority. He would never just sit and let his wife entertain any saying without first interjecting the final word according to truth. He is no sitting duck, but ready on his guard as a man to defend his own. He studies to show himself approved unto God as they talk and read to one another on a daily basis. His friends are those who walk with the Lord and those in need, too. But they all understand who he is and never try his boundaries beyond what he has set for them.

This is a man of God, normal in every way: every day a game here or there, normal friend, normal concerns, and a great sex life, too. He is vocal about his lovemaking and his longing for more of it comes naturally. Wanting only the best for his wife, he asks if everything is okay and if he is pleasing to her. Never too harsh with his wife, but treats her like his eternal last. He has all his needs met and makes sure he takes care of her, so that she is able to care for his needs. He has an awareness of the enemy and has seen his simple tactics, too, but God is his guide and his eyes are hid inside the Word.

These are examples you can be just like and more by simply confessing who you are in God. "Verily, verily, I say unto you, He that believeth on me, the works that I do shall he do also; and greater works than these shall he do; because I go unto my Father. And whatsoever ye shall ask in my name, that will I do, that the Father may be glorified in the Son. If ye shall ask any thing in my name, I will do it" (John 14:12–14). Imagine the *greater works* you could see in yourself and your marriage if you only began to make positive confessions daily.

Tactic 4: DECEIVE AND DEFILE YOU

"Be not deceived; God is not mocked: for whatsoever a man soweth, that shall he also reap."
Galatians 6:7

If you don't understand anything else in life, you need to get this principle down about the devil. He is the founder for the Deception Hall of Fame. While you spend forty to sixty hours a week working, he has spent centuries working to deceive God's creation if possible. We are no match for the devil without the help of Jesus Christ. The devil came and tempted Jesus with all kinds of deceptive wants for the Lord, but Jesus saw right through all his deceptive tricks. He may be deceptive, but he's not smart. He will try the same tactic on each of you still today. Just because it didn't work on Jesus doesn't mean it will not work on somebody. Satan goes around as a roaring lion seeking whom he may devour.

What is deception? It is the practice of deliberately making somebody believe things that are not true. Secondly, it is an act, trick, or device intended to deceive or mislead somebody. A lot of people accuse Eve of being deceived, and I agree. But before we make Eve just a billboard spectacle, let's look at our own deception. Hosea 4:6 (emphasis mine) says, "My people are destroyed for a lack of knowledge: *because thou hast rejected knowledge.*" On a daily basis, we reject what is true about our marriages only to believe a lie. For example, you go to church and the pastor says to confess that you're a conqueror and you repeat, "I am a conqueror."

Then the pastor says to turn and tell at your neighbor, "You are a conqueror!" You look your spouse in her eyes and say, "You are a conqueror," knowing all along in your heart she couldn't conquer anything.

Deception. When you get home, you forget you are married to a conqueror, but instead to a no good, don't want to help you cook or clean or raise the children coward. At least that's what you just said with your heart. When you are deceived, you are made to believe things that are not true. Like a video, the enemy shows you just how bad your marriage really is and that's what you believe. As you open your mouth, what you really feel comes out. But according to Scripture, you should accept what is correct according to the Word of God by faith.

No matter where we are as couples, we must cast down imaginations that exalt themselves above the Word of God or from the pastor. You do a great job of quoting but not meaning what you are saying and the enemy knows this very well, for out of the abundance of your heart comes blessing and cursing. It is not enough to just say what someone tells you to say, it has to become apart of your soul and get connected to your heart. You speak those things which be not as though they were, but in your mind you really believe the faith kind of talk when you are going through, is only for the deep and for real, saved saints. Besides, you may think, they are not married to the person I live with. I have been speaking life forever and now what?

I did that in the beginning of marriage and cannot imagine being the only one to have to keep standing and do all this work until I die. Why not? What happened to the conqueror, what happened to until you die for greater or for worse? What happened to the end of a thing is better than the beginning of a thing? What happened to it's not your power but God's Spirit, saith the Lord? You still think this is all about what you can and cannot do instead of what God is able to do and has already done. Do you really believe the Scripture when God declares, "Eyes hath not seen, nor ear heard, neither have entered into the heart of man, the things which God hath prepared for them that love Him" (1 Corinthians 2:9)? Do you think that deletes your marriage and your sex life? Who has bewitched you?

Before you speak up and make a fool of yourself as if you are not being deceived, take a good hard look at what Satan has had you believing. Every day, you believe your marriage is bad, your spouse is not the best, your husband is cheating, your wife is having an affair, your sex is bogus, your best friend (your spouse) is not the one you sleep with, you don't care about sex but it's all the other person cares about, your marriage is simply hell on earth, there's no way your spouse can get better, you have prayed and nothing's getting better, someone else is finer or better looking than your spouse, and finally, there is nothing wrong with you. The preacher has given you Scriptures on how to get better, make confession, and walk out what you believe, but you didn't study because you assumed he doesn't understand nor live at your house. You are clearly persuaded that if Satan does exist he is living in your spouse, but you haven't done anything about it. Deception.

You never take the time to study the Word and then confess what you have in your spouse. In the beginning, you both said I do and believed God put you together. Well, believe God will be there with you through it all. No matter how bad things are, you should never reject the knowledge or what the Word of God declares by saying, whether verbally or not, "It is not!" So, let me ask you, who is deceived? God is your comforter, strong tower, and most of all, mediator for a lot of the problems that arise in your marriage, and when He gives a word of wisdom, you should receive the word with gladness and endeavor to apply it to your life. But like the children of Israel still in a lot of ways, you focus on the now and not the Word of God; you focus on quick results, covet other people's supposedly nice homes, want your spouse to be super saved, super clean, super groomed, and whatever else you think you need to have that you already have.

Deception (fooling yourself), is a process that takes place deliberately as you fail to uncover the truth that is hidden from you. The enemy has been so great at this that he has managed to fool Christian couples today into believing that what you see is naturally what you get. So many couples today are throwing in the towel before they are even able to see the end of a thing or see God uncover the hidden truth or jewels in a person. You in your own strength are simply just fed up.

You hear the Word in all kinds of ways: TV, church, and your fellow saints, but to try to go home and walk in it in word or deed is hard, you say. But truly in your hearts, you have no understanding on what you are really standing. You spend how much time studying Scriptures about the areas of sex and intimacy in your life and pray and talk to your hubby about sex how many times? You have your own way of understanding sex and how it is supposed to happen in your house. You have never prayed about the sex and intimacy in your marriage.

Oh, you think it's just an act that is supposed to happen. You think you have it all figured out when you are with your wife or husband and you spend no time talking about the needs of the other person. You have a high sex drive and the other person has no sex drive, but you think you must engage in sex without sensuality and make the other person feel uncomfortable. Deceived.

No sex, the wife says. I don't care, whatever. The husband sees adultery becoming more of a reality. Where did all this come from? Your sowing, for whatsoever a man soweth, that shall he also reap. But you didn't sow anything, exactly. Nothing from nothing begets nothing. But just because you aren't sowing doesn't mean the enemy isn't planning for your emptiness. The enemy also plays on your ability to do nothing. So, you don't have to be literally sowing, it can start in your mind. These seeds have been sown through your mind. If you think all day, he is being unfair, selfish, ignorant, and how could he even possibly desire to cheat, you don't value his choice in choosing you, so what does that say about you? You never are satisfied with who you are but you never say anything; it's all a war in your mind. A garden full of seeds you never planted but have polluted your outlook for the one you love and you never opened your mouth.

Then it happens: one argument, then another argument, and another. The very seeds you speak begin to get watered and take root to your soul. Now every day there is something to bother you and seems nagging as you and your spouse try to communicate. Whether you open your mouth or not when confrontation occurs, what you are thinking is growing daily. A quiet mouth doesn't signify a quiet mind. The same way seeds can be sown, they can also be uprooted. You both have to be aware that deception is going to come because it's one of the enemy's greatest tricks in his bag.

But when two people do several things well—communicate with one another in love, are aware of the person they are married to, study to show themselves approved unto God first, walk in right standing with God, and really cherish the mate God has blessed them with—the enemy is not able to just come in with his deceptive ways and destroy their marriage. *If the enemy can keep you both deceived, you will be too blindsided to confess what rightfully belongs to you.* As couples, you have weapons: the Word of God and the power of agreement.

"The word of God is quick, powerful, and sharper than any two-edged sword, piercing even to the dividing asunder of the soul (mind, will, and emotions) and spirit, and of the joints and marrow, and is a discerner of the thoughts and intents of the hearts" (Hebrews 4:12, addition mine). When you want to fight any fight in the spirit realm and win, you must use the Word with an understanding of what you are saying by faith. Be not deceived; you will reap what you are sowing. If you sow love, happiness, respect, and joy, you will get that in return.

But if all you do is that which is unpleasing and disrespectful toward one another, you can believe that is all your marriage and bedroom will be filled with. You can't expect to talk crazy to your spouse all day, be nice to the church members, and then just expect the bedroom to be a bed of roses. Not even a dog scorned will just come up and lick your face unless he is desperate or hungry. Showing love starts with you both speaking, learning, and loving on one another throughout the day as a way of life. You must sow the right words in order to reap a harvest in any area of your life. A good night of sex comes from sowing seeds of love and compassion throughout the day.

Some of the best nights of lovemaking started with my husband making the time throughout the day to minister to me in his words and deeds; for example, a rub on the back while I was cooking, a smile for no reason, a kiss on the forehead, rubbing me when I was really tired, and simply paying attention to all my body language during the day. If my day wasn't going well and I wasn't in the best mood when I got in the bed, it didn't take long for him to figure out I was not into the sex thing that night. The enemy is defeated by what you both say as couples, so it's imperative that you both are saying the same things. One out of step can mean a whole count unnoticed and room for the enemy.

A house divided cannot stand and the enemy knows this. As soon as your bedroom is going through trouble and you cannot agree on the sex part of your life, it is time to humble yourself before the Lord. It's the time to pray specifically about what you are having problems with and then get the Word of God, the Bible, and find what God has to say concerning that area. This is not the time to accuse one another but to be watchful for how the enemy is trying to entrap you. Some Christians are so deceived that if the enemy walked right up in the bedroom of many homes, they would not even recognize him.

They would still think it's about one another or be so upset about the issues that they wouldn't see that the enemy has come in, sown the seed, and been long gone. It is imperative to know your spouse and when you hear things that are not of God and are not coming from your spouse, you turn the light on Satan and rebuke the Spirit. You must learn how to fight the enemy in your bedroom with the Word of God.

Undefiled means not defiled. Defile has several meanings: to corrupt or ruin something; to damage the reputation of someone or a good name; to make a holy or sacred thing or place no longer fit for ceremonial use; and lastly, to make something dirty or polluted. Satan wants your bedroom to be defiled and if that's not bad enough, for you to accept this as normal. Hebrews 13:4 reads, "Marriage is honorable among all, and the bed undefiled, but fornicators and adulterers God will judge." The Message Bible reads, and I really like this translation more, "Honor marriage and guard the sacredness of sexual intimacy between the wife and the husband. God draws a fine line against casual and illicit sex."

When you choose not to honor the sex in your life, you are not honoring marriage or God, who made this act holy. Honor in marriage is not thinking that having sex is just cliché, just a get-by way of living with the one you say you love; that's not honoring marriage. It's having sex just for the sake of personal pleasure and not considering the other person's needs, going through the role-play of having sex and never really enjoying it. Colossians 3:23, quoted all over Christian houses, states, *"do everything as unto to the Lord."* You know the rest, but when it comes to the bedroom, then it's "do everything as you feel or you want to." What happened to the wholeheartedness, as unto the Lord? Is this act not associated with the "everything" in the Scripture?

Most of the time, it's not Satan who has defiled your bedrooms, it's you. You have allowed how you think about sex to defile your bedroom. In your mind, it's just something that you do, but in the mind of Christ it is a way of life and a commandment he ordained for only married people. Be fruitful and multiply by replenishing the earth. To not partake in this act and embrace it as an honorable work is disobedience in the sight of God. Acts 10:15, "...what God hath cleansed, that call not thou common.""Therefore, whether you eat or drink, or whatever you do, do all to the glory of God" (1 Corinthians 10:31). Everything you do, whether it is eating, sleeping, talking, or even sexual intercourse, should be done in such a way that it brings glory and honor to God.

The bedroom requires prayer, discipline, and a degree of dignity; dignity in such a degree that you both respect one another enough to learn to get better, learn to communicate openly about how you feel and then come together and find out what works and what doesn't for the glory of God. So many couples allow the enemy to come in and shame the name of God by making the bedroom scene a place of controversy as if God never had anything to do with it. To me, that is defiled thinking and outright disobedience to the Word of God. Just because you have no desire in it, or maybe you are not the best at what you do, or simply because you don't enjoy your spouse does not mean that is the way that the Lord ordained it to be.

Why do you think so many married couples believe worshipping God on Sunday, evangelizing, and preaching are the only forms in which we are to bring Him glory? Could it be because it is just too easy to do and there is no other person to commune with about how you do what you do? Well, sex is a commandment from God, and when we are sexually active and we enjoy it with our spouse, not only is our marriage better, but God is glorified. Our Father has blessed us with freedom and he declares, "To whom the son has set free is free indeed."

As His children, we have a freedom to enjoy sex that, even though it is physical, as spiritual people, God has allowed us to partake in for one main reason: to be just like Him to create human beings. As a Christian who is married and in line with the will of God for your life, you cannot allow the enemy to corrupt your mind concerning sex. You can't allow something that is supposed to be honorable in the sight of God to become a defilement in your own mind. Sex is a ceremonial act, a time of great honor, a time to bless the name of Jesus for making someone perfect for you to live with while here on earth. Like every other area in your life in which God has gifted you, you should thank God for sex and strive to use it the remainder of your marriage. Abraham and Sarah and many of the matriarchs of the Word of God continued to have sex throughout their time on earth.

Dwight Harvey Small, in *Design for Christian Marriage*, says, "The distinctive thing about the Christian concept of sex is in thus fully acknowledging it as a biological function in man, but at the same time insisting that it is a function of the total personality which at its highest is spiritual. Its physical aspects cannot be disassociated from its spiritual aspects" (pg. 29).

Satan has no power in your bedroom unless you give it to him. The enemy is going to come as a roaring lion and he will throw weapons toward your sexual life, but we are admonished as Christians to continue to pray and resist the devil and he will flee. He will try to annihilate, blindside, control, and most of all, *deceive* you, but when you continue to keep your bedroom lifted up in prayer and communicate with your spouse, all his weapons are silenced. Sex cannot be verbally explained, but when it is performed, mere words need not be expressed.

PRACTICE IT

Some more suggestions on how to defend the enemy from helping you defile your bedroom.

1. Make tonight a special night and take the time to learn about your spouse's body parts. Ask what is what if you seriously don't know. Women are excited about anytime a man takes time to learn the parts of a woman's body. Just be mindful of how you word things.
2. Make sure the room is quiet and listen to what hurts and what heals as you engage in sexual intercourse. If one position hurts, be sensitive enough to know that you may need to change things up a bit. Don't settle for one position just because you have that mastered; learn to explore new positions.
3. Be open to change and be willing to try new things that your partner may be interesting in trying. If you are worried about what's bad or not, remember you both have the Holy Spirit and your conviction is your guide.
4. Ladies, keep your old wives tales to yourself. Men, no woman wants to hear about what your friends do or what you got a glimpse of on TV and desire to do. Come up with your own ideas or research to impress one another. These are your memories and no one else's.
5. When you don't want to have sex, go and pray and ask God to help you to have more of a desire to be pleasing to your spouse. Do this every time until it becomes a routine and your desires change.
6. In your prayer request, keep your bedroom lifted up and pray about receiving a greater understanding concerning you and your lovemaking. Always be transparent when you pray concerning this area. When things are bothering in your bedroom, don't be afraid to pray about them and talk to your spouse about them as soon as possible.
7. Spend time with your spouse naked, engage in conversation while looking into one another's eyes, and being very honest just ask, "Honey, do you think I'm honoring you in marriage?"

Chapter Six

The Rules of Engagement in Sex

We are not the only generation who has had sex problems as Christians. In the book of 1 Corinthians, Paul is writing to the church at Corinth on their sexual problems, and boy did they have sexual problems. In this chapter, we are going to focus on a certain passage of Scripture because it is covered with meat from the Bible for our sexual lives. I choose to write using the Message Bible because the wording is easier to understand for all Christians, young and old.

When you think about rules of engagement, you think of rules for what we are supposed to do or not do, what we are engaging in, etc. In this section, I decided that it was important to address some of the earlier saints and their questions so that we can learn from the counsel Paul gave them on how to simply engage in sex the right way. The apostle Paul wrote back to the church of Corinth for what he believed the rules of engagement for sex in marriage should be. But keep in mind that Paul believed these were his ways of understanding and not any commandments of God. Paul, being an apostle and the overseer for the church at Corinth, only felt it befitting for him to give them spiritual wisdom. As we dig further into this section, you will come to realize that nothing God does or says is out of order, even having sex has a method to the madness.

Let's study 1 Corinthians 7:1–10. These are what I believe are foundational values for Christians regarding sex. Whenever questions arise in your marriage regarding what you can and cannot do, first of all, always pray together. Then begin to ask the Lord: "Do we separate from sex for a season? What is Your view of sex?" And most of all, "Am

I pleasing in my lovers eyes?" Then allow these ten rules to govern your way of thinking in this area.

Rule 1: Take ownership to the statement that it is good to have sex.

"Now, getting down to the questions you asked in your letter
to me. First, is it a good thing to have sexual relations?"
1 Corinthians 7:1

We already know that sex has many advantages when you actually take part in it with your spouse and in agreement. But I believe Paul had to reiterate this to the church because evidently some Corinthians believed it wasn't or it was just something so fleshly that mixed views were being formed. First of all, even with Christians, most people are not waiting to have sex until they get married. When they get married, they are already programmed to see sex a certain way because of past relationships. We all come to marriage with so much sex baggage that it instantly programs our way of thinking and like any other area in our Christian life, we need to renew our minds and accept what is true as our new way of thinking.

In this passage, Paul is trying to help the church at Corinth renew their minds and believe simply that sex is good. But you say you don't understand just how intense things can be in marriage that it makes seem as if sex can simply be done away with; I don't have to understand, God does and so does the one you love. Share your true feelings with your spouse and ask him or her to make this confession a confession for the both of you, "That sex is good!". You will be surprised how many Christians today would never say "sex is good," even married couples. Remember, as Christians we have the power to speak those things as though they are. If you want to see a revival come in your house tonight, walk around in your bedroom for a couple of minutes until it gets into your spirit and say, *"Sex is good!"* As Christians, this is the way we are to view sex. The same way we believe that the Spirit that inspired Paul's writings on having all things that pertaineth to life and are godly is the same Spirit that instructed him to say sex is good.

Rule 2: Be sexually balanced and embrace your sex drive.

> "Certainly—but only within a certain context. It's good for a man to have a wife, and for a woman to have a husband. Sexual drives are strong, but marriage is strong enough to contain them and provide for a balanced and fulfilling sexual life in a world of sexual disorder."
> 1 Corinthians 7:2

Having routine sex is only good when you are married. Here Paul makes no mention of outside affairs and even when he refers to it, he calls it what it is, fornication. The only time we as humans should be enjoying sex is when we are married. Now, he also deals with the fact that these married people were to be one man and one woman, not one man and one man. Why? This is the way we produce our own kind.

Homosexuality has been around for a long time, but even Paul, the father of the Christian movement, is instructing his own church at Corinth to marry a certain way and that was as a man and a woman. Nothing else was even mentioned, wasn't even to be considered as a marriage, or wasn't even a way for the church to survive. If there's one thing the people of this world, including Christians, can understand, it is that we live in a world where the very view of sex is dysfunctional. But Paul is instructing us to be aware that sex drives are strong and as long as you are married, you can contain every desire. You and your spouse have been given the power to fulfill one another in every way by and with the help of God.

Sex drive is a part of our makeup as human beings, and since a lot of people are having premarital sex, even Christians have to learn how to find that balance to make one another happy and live a fulfilling life. See, when you experiment before marriage, it leaves little room for expectations that should come from your spouse.

Today, even some Christian couples live together and have sex before saying I do. When the couple finally decides to get married and live for God, the first thing to go is the very act that put them together. The problem sometimes is that saints believe that now that they are living right for God that anything done in the past including sex, is unholy. Where did this lie come from? The devil, because he wants you to think that since you were walking in the flesh fornicating you must be fornicating now that you are saved, too. Ridiculous, but so many people actually believe sex is bad if you are too sexually active or actually enjoy it. There is nothing sinful about doing something you are supposed to do; it's doing something you are not supposed to do that is wrong. So if you are married now, you can have great sex even though you practiced sex before marriage, just ask God for forgiveness. You are married now and nothing changed about the sex drive, just your understanding of sin.

Welcome and take advantage of the sex drive or in other words, the sexual activity or behavior leading to sex, in each of you because it is not ungodly. In today's society they would like to have you think, that as you age your sex drive will fluctuate so while it is up and going, one should go with the flow and not dismiss it. Your sex drive is simple that, something sexually that has to be controlled, and most of all exercised and what better place than marriage. I truly believe that in all things, saints should pray for long life, an understanding of their spouses sex drive, and for the sex drive to be in operation as long as the Lord would allow. Your husband's longing can be fulfilled by you meeting his needs and vice versa. God desires that we be balanced in all things and especially concerning sex.

Rule 3: The marriage bed is a place of mutuality.

> "The marriage bed must be a place of mutuality—the
> husband seeking to satisfy his wife, the wife seeking to satisfy
> her husband."
> 1 Corinthians 7:3

Just this Scripture by itself is a mouthful. When you get married, it's no longer a "just-you" way of thinking to a certain degree. Now that you are married, Paul is instructing you to understand that the bedroom is a place of agreement. It's not the place where you get to have it your way and that's it. If you want it your way, get up out the bed and go to Burger King. The Bible powerfully declares in Amos that two cannot walk except they be agreed. If the bedroom is supposed to be the place we lay down to rest and wake up rejuvenated, and then in the middle of all that, sex takes place, then I can understand some people becoming disappointed when they are not able to get the proper sleep.

But even in that, it's still no reason to be evil and refuse to have sex with your spouse every night. Guess what? How do you expect the person to wake up and walk? You both may need to start getting in the bed early enough to enjoy this act. If you keep going too long without it, you will understand why so many married people are walking around snappy, mean, frowning, and just snaky. You may not get your way at the bank or your way on the freeway driving home, but in your bedroom it should not be a "mine" but an "ours" that takes place.

The bedroom is supposed to be that place where you both walk in agreement, giving up some of the No's for Yeses and sacrifice for one another to ensure you go to bed with a smile. No one is promised tomorrow, and if waiting for tomorrow is always your excuse, you have no clue when the Lord will call you or your spouse home. Ask God to help you make every night purposeful and for you to live it as if it was your last night together.

I believe some of the happiest people are the ones who have a healthy and balanced life of sex and intimacy. These are the people who not only practice great sex, but they spend time learning and getting to know one another. They value the bedroom and don't allow anger or disagreements to get a foot in their bedroom or marriage. They value waking up with one another as if it was the last day. Even if you don't manage to have the greatest sex every night, you know how to stroke one another's egos, massage, cuddle, or maybe just listen or be there when the other person is in need. You may be upset but you don't get ridiculous in your disagreeing but show love and listen to the other person side as well. The marriage bed is a place all by itself that no one else has access to but you and your spouse. It's the special place no one can relate to or even give any opinion about. It's the one thing that God said to keep holy and let nothing, not even yourself, defile. "Let nothing defile your bedroom."

Your bedroom is where you find the joy of one another and learn the secrets of your loved one, but at the same time, leave them there. Where you give in to win and give up in order to make peace. The bedroom is where the ability to be humble is birthed and the courage to lead still reigns supreme. In power is power dethroned, as you realize no one is in charge and you both take orders from one another. This is a place of total unison and complete submission to one another.

Rule 4: Be Humble

"Marriage is not a place to 'stand up for your rights.' Marriage is a decision to serve the other, whether in bed or out." 1 Corinthians 7:4

The Bible declares that the husband's body belongs to the wife and the wife belongs to the husband, but ultimately you both belong to God. When you give your life to Christ, you take on his likeness and his newness. He comes to live inside of you. What you do with your body you do with God. When Joseph was accused of sinning, he said he could not lay with Potipher's wife because he would sin against God. It is a humbling experience each time you sleep with your spouse knowing that this is a vessel appointed and chosen by God.

So there are so many people in the world, right? But you are only married to one person. God created a person just for you who he predestined before the foundations of the world. Many are called but few are chosen, and you have to realize the one you are laying with was specially chosen for you. Being married is a gift that many take for granted, especially being able to bring pleasure to one another. When you stand up for Jesus, you invite Jesus to be in control, but when you allow yourself and flesh to get in the way, you will always fall short in your bedroom.

Each time you desire to please your wife or husband, you must realize it's not even about pleasing each other, but it's about pleasing the God on the inside of yourselves. Whatever my husband asks, that I will do. I am obedient to the anointing in his life and I respect the God in him. I lost my rights to think and act on my own when it comes to the bedroom when I said I do because we are now one. Whatever we do, we do because we want to love and cherish one another on top of bringing glory to our Father. "How can we continue to walk, except we be agreed" (Amos 3:3).

Rule 5: There is no such thing as no sex without each other's consent.

"Abstaining from sex is permissible for a period of time if you both agree to it, and if it's for the purposes of prayer and fasting—but only for such times. Then come back together again. Satan has an ingenious way of tempting us when we least expect it." 1 Corinthians 7:5

This rule should probably be the first rule in the list and, most of all, a warning when people get married. The problem here is that Paul, like many seasoned sexual people, understands that until you have control over your mind, sex is powerful. It is not like something you can just turn on and turn off until you have disciplined yourself. If you are used to having sexual relations with your spouse all the time and then they stop, your own body begins to wonder what's going on. So many couples don't understand that sex is the glue, but not the cement, in marriage, but it still helps the couples stick together. Men need sex and women need affection. As discussed earlier, sex has all kinds of great qualities that a man needs and to withhold sex from a man for too long can lead to frustrations and unnecessary stress in his life.

Satan has been around since dirt was made, and he fully understands the timing of tempting couples when you are not sexually active. No, not just sexually active, but making love together. Sex allows the two of you to close gaps that may have crept in through the day. It allows each of you to arouse and awaken the desire to be with one another even the more. It keeps the heat and passion burning so there is no other. But the minute you think you don't have to have sex, you have neglected a very important rule in your marriage and it is just a matter of time before the enemy begins to plan his attack. Don't be fooled by Satan; you may think he isn't keeping number when you and your husband are together, but he is and as soon as you reach zero, he will be there.

So cover your bedroom. Keeping count isn't necessary, just make sure you both are satisfied and realize the importance of meeting one another's sexual needs. If problems arise such that you cannot have sex, be sincere and ask your loved one to pray while you refrain and then ask him or her to give you a few days. But when your time is over, you owe it to yourself first of all and then you owe it to your husband or wife to come back and seal that opened door.

Rule 6: Wisdom comes from God; use it when sexual issues arise.

> "I'm not, understand, commanding these periods of abstinence—only providing my best counsel if you should choose them." 1 Corinthians 7:6

The Bible declares that, in all our getting, we should get an understanding. But most of all, we should seek wise counsel. Now where else would the church of Corinth go for this? They had all kinds of crazy to ask, but no matter how crazy, they were not too embarrassed to ask. It's funny today how so many couples call everybody and their mom who have no fruits from a great relationship for advice. Paul tells us that God is not commanding these abstinences, but I am. When sexual problems arise, and they will, get professional help. Stop being afraid, embarrassed, and most of all, too pompous to ask a leader to help you regarding your sexual shortcomings. Yes, your bedroom is secret, but it's okay to enlist men and women of God who are seasoned to help you concerning this area. But pray and look for the fruits in their marriage before you share your diary too soon. Most of all, take your concerns to the Father and let him know exactly what's on your mind.

Rule 7: Marriage is a gift and celibacy is not for everyone.

> "Sometimes I wish everyone were single like me—a simpler life in many ways! But celibacy is not for everyone any more than marriage is. God gives the gift of the single life to some, the gift of the married life to others." 1 Corinthians 7:7

It's sad to see our own clergy being ridiculed in the papers and on the news today because of bad sex allegations, but even that is addressed in these words. Whether you are single or not, you still have to realize that sex is good. When you oppose it, be ready to harness the sleeping dragon in your body called the sex drive. Be ready to understand that Paul is preaching here on being married and how important and good it is to be actively involved in sex with one another, but if you are not married, then be like him—but make sure you are called by God to be single. Otherwise, the sexual desires will find you out and hunt you like a dog. What you do in the dark while lying to yourself and saying, "that sex is horrible in the light," will find you out. You think life is good, no sex is good. If you have never partaken in sex, this scripture is not written to encourage you to get busy trying it out but to know the path you are to live in this life. God will keep the single man or woman, if he calls you to the single life and Paul even goes so far as to saying this life is simpler. Whether you are married or single, the mandate to carry out either act has to be confirmed by God. Through prayer, self evaluation, and desires to be with someone or not be with another human being, is a starting point on finding out the path you should take in this journey toward living.

Rule 8: If you're single, stay single, but be led by God.

"I do, though, tell the unmarried and widows that singleness might well be the best thing for them, as it has been for me."
1 Corinthians 7:8

Not everyone can live the single life. If God has called you to live the single life, praise the Lord! But be not deceived, God is not mocked. If you say you are going to live a single life, it has to be a life lived totally for God. For whatever you entertain as a single will definitely entertain you. We are in the last days; men and women are losing natural affections toward one another. As a single, you have to be careful that you are not operating in this spirit, but you are truly being led to live the single life. Single life has its own hard comings. Not everyone can be like Paul, but we all can strive to be Christlike. Most of all, wait on God to prepare you for your mate. If you're wondering what's taking such a long time, think about how detailed you are and then just praise God for leading and guiding you to your spouse.

Rule 9: Marriage brings balance to your soul.

"But if they can't manage their desires and emotions, they should by all means go ahead and get married. The difficulties of marriage are preferable by far to a sexually tortured life as a single." 1 Corinthians 7:9

For some Christians, marriage is like a jigsaw puzzle. Couples struggle to find the pieces to bring the picture together as to why they married each other. But the missing piece to the puzzle is simply understanding that neither of you can put the puzzle together alone. A good sex life breathes balance.

If you are overworked, tired, underworked, bored, or even spiritually exhausted, it will begin to affect your total man. When your soul is out of sync, it is just a matter of time before the body follows. If you have a willing spouse who can help you dwell together according to knowledge and learn from one another through the good and bad, the married life really does get easy.

It's so sad to see married couples throwing in the towel early or even after some years of being married. For years as a single, you would've killed to be with the person and now you can't stand to look at your wife or husband. Sad. Thank God for marriage, as it is the closing of one chapter in your life and an endless story of the both of you. When you were single and desired a mate, you had to entertain all kinds of thoughts, some self-inflicted and some simply just part of being single. But when you get married, this is supposed to be a time of refreshing. A time where it's not just one person working, but the both of you.

Rule 10: Divorce is not an option.

"And if you are married, stay married. This is the Master's command, not mine." 1 Corinthians 7:10

So many people ask me how in the world my marriage is so successful and I must admit, besides the anointing of God, it is our family vision. It is not enough to just recite vows, eat wedding cake, and have fun on your wedding day because when all of that is over, you wake up with someone to whom you already may say, "Can you please stop snoring?" I came to realize that marriage is something that is going to require every part of you as a human being and complete honesty. The Bible declares that God's people have perished for a lack of understanding and no vision. Knowing that, my husband and I have plastered the family vision on our front wall entrance as a reminder of why we are together. If there is any question as to why each of us is still here when angers flare, we both need to read the vision. Not only is this marriage for the both of us, it is a commitment we have both made unto God. If we say we love God and we know He loves us because He died for us, I could not imagine going back on a commitment to Him.

I have had many nights where I just wanted to leave and as soon as I got to the door. Then, I cry after reading why I was still there. See, I realized when my husband and I sat down to write our vision that we really wanted to be together for life, but the harsh everyday trials can really work your nerves. That's why when we wrote our vision, we were honest with our emotions and made it plain that we may hurt each other, but we have to learn how to forgive and remember our love was bigger than the trial. In writing this vision, we realized that we owed it to ourselves to keep our commitment to our God first and then to one another.

Quitting would never be an option because we value the seeds that we both have sown into one another. I made a vow to my husband that I would never start over on what we have built and he has vowed to forever be there to help shape and mold me to be the woman I am supposed to be. It is his responsibility for me to make it and I am holding him responsible. My husband is the head and God is a God of order in marriage. When problems arise, allow God to speak with the head and as a woman, take your place in prayer and fasting that God gets his message to your spouse for the whole family. If at anytime you feel you become the head, you will always struggle to see your husband in a place of authority in your marriage. Because the man is to be the head of any home, this still does not validate the woman to be and do whatever she wants, but to walk in submission and unison with the family vision and man of God. Some of the most successful marriages have all to do with: a woman who is able to humble herself and allow God to birth out her husband.

Marriage has to be the most costly investment you make, and you have to realize that there is no such thing as a receipt in marriage or a deal gone bad. With every market crash, this economy still manages to spend billions, and with everything else in life, marriage is the very epitome of our Father. When we walk in unison, we become just like him: Father, Son, and Spirit; Man, Woman, and God. It's perfect, and it is what our Father has mandated from the foundations of this earth. When you get married and believe God has put you together, nothing, not even you, shall separate what God has put together. Divorce is not an option when you have a vision and you both can run with it and hold one another accountable for bringing it to pass.

Morning Prayer

As much as you can remember, wake up and pray over your beloved, from the top of the head down to the toes, that every part of his or her body would be in full operation and pleasing in your sight as well as God's. Pray your husband become the lord in your home while our Lord and Savior works through him. Begin to pray for humility in your wife and a spirit of patience to invade the house. Ask God to strengthen him if he is weak, heal her if she hurts, and most of all, show you how to place yourself in a way that he or she would learn to love you even more. Ask God to show you how to be more creative when it comes to making love, kissing, touching, and most of all, just being intimate with the one you love.

Ask God to reveal to you what it really means to be in love with your spouse. Don't be afraid to go naked and unashamed before the Father and say what you don't like about yourself and ask him to renew in your mind about your body. If God doesn't speak, that means you are to keep waiting, praying, and accept that nothing is wrong with you and that you simple need to accept things as they are. Ask God to teach you how to work what you have and enjoy your spouse while you are blessed to be with them. Pray God renews your mind concerning the way you have thought about sex, have engaged in sex, and your way of thinking about your spouse thus far. Confess that divorce is not an option and your best days are ahead, and as a matter of fact, they are upon you right now. You are ready, charged, and engaged in the things that are pleasing to your spouse and you are ready for love.

Chapter Seven

The Art of Building True Love

"There is a way which seemeth right unto a man but the end thereof are the ways of death." Proverbs 14:12

As married couples, there is only one way to think, one way to live, and one way to love: through Christ. Okay, I can hear each of you saying amen. But I know what you are already thinking: "I already know this." Let me be the first to say I'm glad you do because you should have no problem understanding this parable. For many Christians, we live our day-to-day lives in church, praying, and even fasting, but we never get rid of our own stinking thinking. We say we are living for Christ, but truly we are still self-centered in a lot of ways, ways that are truly affecting ourselves as well as our marriages.

For years, we have been married to ourselves and we have become programmed to think a certain way, but have we really died to self and our own domineering way of living? Even some of the most devout Christian are subject to self temptations and shortcomings if they are not careful to study daily and put themselves in the hands of God. God wants to give us a new behavior and way of thinking when it comes to marriage and sex. If you think you are going to keep thinking the same and never succumb to God's way of thinking concerning you and your marriage, you are in for a long, hard road ahead.

"I am able to do nothing from myself (independently, of my own accord, but only as I am taught by God and as I get His order). Even as I hear, I judge (I decide as I am bidden to decide, as the voice comes to me, so I give a decision), and my judgment is right (just, righteous), because I do not seek or consult my own will (I have no desire to do what is pleasing to myself, my own aim, my own purpose) but only the will and pleasure of the Father who sent me" (John 5:30, Amplified).

How can we get better, how can we build love, how we can we climb mountains and reach higher heights in our bedroom but by chasing after God like we are going out of our minds? Jesus Christ himself declared that he was nothing without God and without his Father's leadings. How do we live great lives in our marriages but by being led by the Spirit? The Spirit speaketh expressly to us, if we are listening and if we desire to live a life truly controlled by Him—in all aspects. You cannot afford to try and turn God on and off when you want to; no, God has to be an ever-abiding presence that is evident in our lives. Married people have missed it when they believe they have become married only to lose themselves. No, the process of losing oneself started the day you gave your life to the Lord.

I believe a lot of times Christian marriages try to literally own one another and this is clearly not the will of the Father. We really do think our spouses are our responsibility, the way they act has to do with us, and that we are responsible for change in their lives; it is God who wills to do things in the life of Christians. We don't even have the keys to our own souls; God bought us with a precious price and He expects us to live according to His statutes and leadings. How do we figure we can build and make a difference in our marriages if the true source is secretly ourselves? Psalm 127:1 declares, "Except the Lord builds the house, they labor in vain who build it."

God wants us to walk in the Spirit, seek His face diligently, and hunger and thirst after him and then He has promised to fill our cup until it overflows. He has promised to reign in every area of our lives and give us the desires of our hearts, whatever they are, according to His will. With that being said, is sex his will? Is lovemaking, or whatever you want to call it, in His will? Absolutely. It is the desire of our Father that we prosper and be in good health. Prosper means all things—your sex life, finances, relationships, jobs, and every area of your life—would bear fruit as you yield and submit your total being to the One who sent you. Jesus repeatedly said He can do nothing of Himself, unless the Father wills him to do it; he was absolutely lost without His father.

This type of thinking is where we need to be spiritually. Abiding in the presence of the Lord at all times to the point where we lose consciousness of self and become fully engulfed with God's Spirit. "Dwell in me, and I will dwell in you. (Live in me, and I will live in you.) Just as no branch can bear fruit of itself without abiding in (being vitally united to) the vine, neither can you bear fruit unless you abide in me" (John 15:4–5, addition mine). So here is the secret to the art of true love: what you desire from your spouse you will have to go through God to get.

You cannot get anything from your marriage the Lord doesn't give you: if you want more love, keep abiding; if you want great sex, keep abiding; if you want peace, keep abiding. Whatever it is you are hungering and thirsting for in your marriage, God is saying, "Hunger and thirst after me and you shall be filled."

Let the Church say, Amen!

References Page

Meyers, Joyce. I dare you. Embrace life with passion. New York, NY. Faith Words, 2007

Small, Dwight H. Design for Christian Marriage Old Tappan, NJ, Spire, 1971, pp 92-93.

Sumrall, Lester. *60 Things God Said About Sex.* New Kensington, Penn.: Whitaker House, 1993.

(1999). *Comparative Study Bible.* Grand Rapids, Mic: Zondervan.

Special Invitation
105 Ways to Spice up Your Sex Life Tonight!

You will be surprised how the small details can ruin a perfectly romantic day or night. Here are 105 ways to avoid messing up your sexual desire, as well as adding a little spice to your night!

Ladies:
1. Put on the Victoria's Secret Barely There panties and bra set, rub down in oil, and lay on the bed.
2. Take time to get a pedicure and manicure to ensure soft hands and feet. Play footsie in bed.
3. Focus on how your lips and skin feel to you. Are they soft and supple or dry and cracked?
4. Invest in a good body oil to put on your skin while you are wet after a shower. Make sure the smell is not loud.
5. Invest in fruity lip glosses your husband likes and keep them near you.
6. Brush your teeth and tongue prior to bed, before any face-to-face time, and throughout your day.
7. Take a cool shower, rub down with fruit-smelling lotion, and get in bed naked.
8. Place a saucer of the fruit you smell like in front of you, get in bed, and leave a note: "Dessert."
9. Buy five night pieces to wear with your husband this week. Mix and match is fine, just get his attention.
10. Never go to bed with too much perfume, just something light and sexy. But each night, put it on.

11. Start a thirty-minute routine of working out during the day; it will help your sex life at night.
12. Take a yoga class to learn how to stretch. This prepares you to be more limber in bed and more.
13. Practice Kegel exercises throughout the day, as they strengthen your vaginal walls.
14. Invest in a good sex education book on sex positions. Find one you like and tell your hubby you want to try it. Make sure you pray together about it.
15. For fifteen minutes each day, pray that you are pleasing your husband and if not, ask God to help you.
16. While your husband is asleep, get some anointing oil and rub him down from top to bottom. Be careful! But pray over his whole body. If he wakes, insist he sleep while you continue.
17. One Friday a month, dress up in sexy clothes and go out to dinner with your spouse—don't forget the underclothes; you have to be on point after dinner. Everything has to be like the first time.
18. Surprise your husband with a new sheet set with 1000 or more thread count. Invest in at least two sets.
19. Purchase your husband some new underwear to wear to bed only, about five microfiber or silk sets.
20. Get a robe that has his name engraved on it: "The King" or "My Gardner" (Song of Solomon).
21. Make sure you bathe each night and especially during times of PMS. Our bodies produce more hormones during this time that produce bodily odors. Vaginas have a natural smell, but it shouldn't be a fishy smell.
22. Always have hard candy or a very small goody basket beside your bed. Make sure you got the chap stick. This will help whenever last minute kisses come, fresh breath and moisturized lips enhance kissing.
23. Don't be afraid to wear a little something naughty tonight. Be creative and allow him to live in expectation.

24. Role play is exciting: explore your creative side. Be the nurse or the massage therapist tonight, naked or dressed to undress.
25. Learn how to express yourself during lovemaking. Tell him how great he is or how he makes you feel during sex.
26. Go get a salt or sugar scrub at a local spa or order one from Mary Kay.
27. Schedule a lunch date with your spouse and make it in your bedroom: A variety platter and you in sexy lingerie, lip gloss, and sweet smells with music (one hour max). Plan to do this as a surprise and not routinely.
28. Before sex and foreplay, ask God to give you a creative spirit and a desire to make lovemaking fun.
29. Go on a date during the day. Put on a sundress, smell great, and look good. Tell your husband ten reasons why he is the entire man one woman will ever need. When he leaves, leave a card in the seat of his car, spray with perfume, and say, "Can't wait 'til were together again."
30. Make a lovemaking cd, put it in his vehicle on Monday morning, and say, "Whenever you are having a bad moment today, come listen to this. It will help you to relax your mind. I love you."
31. Pick your husband up for lunch, look extra sweet, and go share a banana split. Demand he meet with you or else. Don't talk bills, children, or anything else; just tell him how much you love spending time with him.
32. Put on his t-shirt, pop some popcorn, get the g-string or new panties, and watch a movie after you put the children to sleep. The goal: quality time together.
33. Take a long bath, get some rest, order Chinese food, set the table, and tell your husband, "Eat, and I'll be waiting when you finish." Spend this day resting, sleeping, and praying for a night of great sex.
34. Write seven notes to your spouse on why he's the absolute best and put them everywhere, even the office.

35. Surprise your husband at work with a basket filled with heart-healthy granola bars, dried fruit, and little snacks to ensure he's always at his best for you.
36. Go for a long ride after church, bring a blanket, and plan it close to the evening to watch the moon rise.
37. Help your husband complete a house project without saying one word or complaining.
38. Leave a white rose and a sexy picture of yourself in the seat of your husband's car. Put a sticky note on it that says, "I already miss you!"
39. Call and have lunch delivered to your spouse with dessert. Note attached: "You are my CEO!"
40. Put together a man's night to affirm his friends and show you don't mind sharing him with his buddies and tell him you'll be back in three hours!
41. Put together a photo book of yourself for his eyes only.
42. Undress your hubby when he comes home and run his bathwater. While he is in the tub, ask him if he would like his dinner and favorite book. Give him his time to relax and unwind.
43. Drop your children off for the night, get a hotel room, and renew your vows with one another: plan dinner, a dessert, and a time to pray for the both of you and the night ahead. Ask God to renew your commitments with one another.
44. Go get a makeover for yourself and meet your hubby and children for dinner without him seeing you until it's done.
45. Start lunch dating again and meet your husband in different places with different looks and smells each time. Always dress to impress.
46. Spend your morning in prayer with your husband. Even if it's just five minutes, start somewhere.
47. Go out and buy your husband his favorite team jersey during the season and ask him to teach you a few things about his favorite sport. Be patient and willing to learn, as boring as it may be.
48. Pray and ask your husband if it's okay for you and him to rest for an agreed amount of time and not have sex. After

this time, you will come back even more refreshed and ready. Keep your promises.
49. Fix your husband's favorite meal and go to the park, invite some of his friends, and don't tell him anything.
50. Prepare a fruit salad and get some whipped cream and some caramel. Tell your hubby that dessert is prepared for him later. Once the children are sleep, get the fruit salad and tell your husband to give you ten minutes in the room alone while you set up the whole table on your body. (Leave the salad out to be room temperature or you will be uncomfortable the whole time.)

Men:

1. Say "I love you, honey" as soon as you get up and let your wife hear this every morning.
2. Make sure you don't have rough, fuzzy hair to aggravate your wife when she lies next to you. If you have to shave prior to getting into the bed for the night, do it.
3. Make sure you brush your teeth and tongue and floss every night. Bad breath kills sex at night.
4. During your lovemaking, express openly exactly how you feel by moans, signs, or even facial gestures.
5. Take the time to learn how to find the most comfortable positions for your wife so she can enjoy you.
6. Make sure you have several pairs of underwear that you only wear to bed. Silk boxers, microfiber underpants, and spandex cotton feel great next to a woman's skin.
7. Spray a little cologne around your back and neck areas. We can't resist a good smell from a man.
8. 90 percent of your lovemaking has to be foreplay, so start early during the day.
9. Take the time to treat your wife to a surprise date. Just tell her the time and place and then pick her up. Make sure you look your best, as if you were meeting for the first time.
10. Every now and then do something that totally blows your woman's mind, but always pray first!

11. Allow your wife to take the day off and instruct her to rest only. Insist you have everything under control.
12. Call your wife throughout the day just to ask how she is and tell her how much you appreciate her.
13. Just do the very thing she has been nagging you to do. It's holding up your sex tonight.
14. Plan a romantic day just for the two of you and let her have no part in the planning. Keep it simple.
15. Leave a note on the mirror when she wakes up and simply say, "Honey, thank you for all you have done, are going to do, and continue to do to make our house a home.
16. Take some oil, pray over it, and while your wife is sleeping, just rub it all over her body. Insist she remain asleep and whatever you do, don't try to make love. Just pray and rub. Then go to bed.
17. Ask your wife if she would take the time to show you what part of her body feels great when you touch her during lovemaking. Have her to place your hands or manly muscle where she feels she needs it the most.
18. Send the children out with your wife for an hour. While she's gone, change the sheets, get a towel and some oil, clean the room, and get pen and paper. Hang a sign on the back of the door (so the children can't see) that reads, "The School of Sex Education." Later that night, let her know how you would love for her to teach you exactly what she wants you to know about what makes her feel incredible during your lovemaking. And if she doesn't know, "tonight we'll learn together."
19. Take the time to learn about your wife's body changes and how they affect the both of you. Reaffirm her that you desire to understand what she may be experiencing when her body is going through changes.
20. Find out what is sexy about your wife and tell her that. Complimenting your wife earns brownie points.
21. Beat your wife home from work, take over dinner, clean the kitchen, shower, spray a little cologne, and get into bed. Let her take care of the children, but you can help. *Don't expect*

anything, kiss her goodnight, and when she wakes up in the morning, leave a card that says, "I do understand your roles as a wife and I love you for all you do."

22. Invite your wife to come have lunch with you at your office. She can bring the food on her way in. Subs and cheesecake slices are perfect!
23. Tell your wife how much you look forward to seeing her face and how her presence makes work easier.
24. When the alarm clock goes off, have a warm, clean towel ready for her to wash her face, a cup of coffee, and a muffin. Tell her, "Honey, wash your face; I want you to be able to see what I see when I look at you. Get a handheld mirror and tell her, "You are the most beautiful woman God ever created and he gave you to me. Here is a little something for my gift from God. Good morning, baby."
25. If your wife isn't feeling well, take the time to take care of her. Then get your Bible and read healing Scriptures all over her. Run bathwater if you have to, but speak life to your wife with an urgency and expectation in mind. Assure her you are there to meet her needs.
26. Take the time to sit down and just talk to your wife before she goes to bed and the children are asleep.
27. Ask your wife if there any concerns that she would like for you to pray about with her.
28. Ask your wife, "Sweetheart, am I pleasing in your eyes? If not, can you please help me to be a better man?" Before she speaks, ask her to pray about what she is going to say and to cover your heart so that you would be in a place to receive it. Assure her that when she speaks you are listening.
29. If your wife always has stuff for you to do as soon as you walk in, grab her hands, kiss her, and say, "Baby, I just walked in and I need about twenty minutes just to gather myself, but I will help you in any way."
30. If your wife is cooking dinner and the children have came home from school, or maybe you're always in the car going to practice, pull over and pronounce the blessing and pray

over the rest of the evening. Demand that God be in total control of you, your wife, and the children.
31. Before you go to work, take the time to go pray and hold each one of your children and tell them how wonderful they are to you and how for them to do their best in school brings you honor as a parent.
32. Tonight before you go to bed, walk through your house and lay hands and pray over every child and all their belongings. Get in the habit of letting your children, and especially your wife, hear you praying for the whole family.
33. If your wife just finished a big event, send her to get a back massage.
34. Learn to listen to your wife's body language during the day; it speaks louder than her words.
35. Ask your wife to go shopping with you to Victoria's Secret and tell her what you would love to see her in and what looks good on her. You don't have to look else where when you can have it all at home.
36. Invest in a Victoria's Secret card for your wife and surprise her with it. Tell her, "Because seeing you in these clothes takes me to another level each time. I love you, baby."
37. Take the time tonight to pray and then ask your wife what makes her happy. You don't have to answer, just listen and pray. Tell her that you are going to get better.
38. If your wife deals with insecurity, ask her to pray for self-confidence in God. Reassure her that if you wanted someone else, God would have set it up that way. If she still feels insecure, tell her God makes no mistakes and to not trust you is to not trust God.
39. Go out on a date night with your wife. Help your wife find a babysitter and insist you both just enjoy one another's company. This night does not have to end in sex, but tell her how much you just want to spend time getting to know her.
40. Learn how to have foreplay the right way by asking your wife what feels good when you touch her.

41. Open your mouth during sex so that she feels comfortable about what you both are doing.
42. As you move, ask her if this is okay, or is that too much or too little. But whatever you do, involve your wife during sex by being more in tune with her reactions to your body parts touching her.
43. Take the time to learn how to enjoy your wife without always having to penetrate something. It may be rubbing in a certain way, maybe her leg or hand on you, but learn other ways that your wife can satisfy you without penetration.
44. Insist that neither of you number every time you make love, but keep track of the days you both enjoyed your lovemaking.
45. Surprise your wife for lunch. Come home with food and chocolates and then ask her to just come and lay near you. Ask her how she is doing and if anything is weighing on her mind that you need to help her pray about.
46. Practice being able to lie near or with your wife without always having to expect something in return; she will love you for this.
47. Let your wife know what really turns you on and why this or that works better than something else.
48. Find out why she doesn't like sexy clothes and perfumes at night. If she is allergic to something, get something that doesn't bother her. If you want her to smell a little sweet, ask her what she likes and buy it.
49. Before you have sex, pray about God allowing the both of you to be totally free in bed and that whatever may be hindering you would be exposed and the bedroom would not be defiled.
50. If your wife doesn't like sex, begin to pray daily and ask God to help her with this. Not at night, but plan a lunch so there is no suggestion of sex. Then ask her why she doesn't like sex and be ready for her answer.
51. If there is pain, first of all tell her, "I am your husband and I don't what you to hurt when we are together because I love you." Ensure her that sex is for the both of you to have

pleasure in and when she is not enjoying it, then you are not.
52. Take a picture of you and your wife and put it in your Bible, at work, and wherever else you deal with temptation and ask that God would cover your thoughts as well as your emotions while you and your wife expose open areas in your marriage.
53. Demand that the Lord would keep his hedge of protection around you and your wife while healing takes place in the bedroom. Pray earnestly while your wife shares her heart about your bedroom and ask God to remove any ounce of pride that would sabotage it.
54. Compliment your wife if she goes out her way to look good for you or an event. Never be the last man to compliment your wife, but the first. Women take compliments to heart when they are spoken.
55. If you ever have problems with noise in the bed, make a pallet on the floor, lock the door, and camp out like old times. Crack the window, grab some midnight goodies and get an old flashlight. If you really wanted your wife to flip out, you might actually make a real tent out of the covers, just to bring the kid side out of both of you.

Remember, marriage is about making memories, and the memories which are remembered the most, are the ones you least expect to happen! Dive in and have fun, let your creative side come alive....

Join us for books II and III of the *Keep It Hot* Series

Printed in the USA
CPSIA information can be obtained
at www.ICGtesting.com
CBHW031711091223
PP14715900002B/1